Routledge Revivals

Egypt

First published in 1985, this study, focusing on Egypt, looks at the underlying reasons why certain political, economic and social events have taken place in the country's history. It provides vital analysis of the political and economic issues of the country, and those that have affected it, as well as providing statistical material on all the key data of the political economy.

The book was originally published as part of the Middle East Research Institute (MERI) Reports on the Middle East which quickly established themselves as the most authoritative and up-to-date information on the state of affairs in the region.

Egypt
MERI Report

Middle East Research Institute

First published in 1985
by Croom Helm

This edition first published in 2015 by Routledge
2 Park Square, Milton Park, Abingdon, Oxon, OX14 4RN
and by Routledge
711 Third Avenue, New York, NY 10017

Routledge is an imprint of the Taylor & Francis Group, an informa business

© 1985 Middle East Research Institute

The right of the Middle East Research Institute to be identified as author of this work has been asserted by him in accordance with sections 77 and 78 of the Copyright, Designs and Patents Act 1988.

All rights reserved. No part of this book may be reprinted or reproduced or utilised in any form or by any electronic, mechanical, or other means, now known or hereafter invented, including photocopying and recording, or in any information storage or retrieval system, without permission in writing from the publishers.

Publisher's Note
The publisher has gone to great lengths to ensure the quality of this reprint but points out that some imperfections in the original copies may be apparent.

Disclaimer
The publisher has made every effort to trace copyright holders and welcomes correspondence from those they have been unable to contact.

A Library of Congress record exists under LC control number: 85004136

ISBN 13: 978-1-138-90200-8 (hbk)
ISBN 13: 978-1-315-69757-4 (ebk)
ISBN 13: 978-1-138-90223-7 (pbk)

MERI REPORT

EGYPT

Middle East Research Institute
University of Pennsylvania

CROOM HELM
London • Sydney • Dover, New Hampshire

© 1985 Middle East Research Institute
Croom Helm Ltd, Provident House, Burrell Row.
Beckenham, Kent BR3 1AT

Croom Helm Australia Pty Ltd, First Floor,
139 King Street, Sydney, NSW 2001, Australia

British Library Cataloguing in Publication Data

Egypt. – (MERI report)
 1. Egypt
 I. MERI II. Series
 962'.055   DT46

 ISBN 0-7099-3551-X

Croom Helm, 51 Washington Street, Dover,
New Hampshire 03820, USA

Library of Congress Cataloging in Publication Data
applied for.

Printed and bound in Great Britain by
Antony Rowe Ltd., Chippenham

TABLE OF CONTENTS

I. Background

1. Geography	3
2. Climate	3
3. Population	3
4. Resources	4
5. Social Structure	5
6. Religion	5
7. Military	6
8. Economic Structure	7
9. Infrastructure	7
10. Social Services	8

II. Political Analysis

1. Summary Conclusions	11
1.1 The President	11
1.2 The Government	11
1.3 Threats to Stability	12
1.4 The Opposition	12
1.5 The Military	12
1.6 The Economy	12
1.7 Relations with Israel	12
1.8 Relations with the Arabs	13
1.9 Relations with the Soviets	13
1.10 Relations with the Unites States	13
1.11 Regional Security Issues	14
2. Political Structure	15
2.1 Political Institutions	15
2.2 Leadership	16
2.3 The Military	17
Politicization	17
Military Structure	18
2.4 Religious Affairs	19
Structure of Islamic Authority	19
Shaikh ot al-Azhar	19
The Mufti	19
The Ministry of Religious Endowments	20
The Muslim Brotherhood	20
The Sufi Sects	20
Resurgent Islam	21
The Copts	22

2.5	Social Structure	22
	Entrepreneurs	23
	Religious Reaction	23
2.6	Factors for Stability and Instability	24

3. Internal Developments 27
    3.1 The Nasser Years 27
    3.2 Transition to Sadat 28
    3.3 Sadat Takes Control 29
    3.4 The Crackdown on Dissent 30
    3.5 Mubarak Comes to Power 32
    3.6 Experiments in Democracy 34
    3.7 Political Parties 35
        The NDP 36
        The Wafd 36
        Strength of the Religious Right 37
        Fragmentation 37
        The Left 38
        1984 Election Results 38

4. Relations with Israel 41
    4.1 Background 41
    4.2 Camp David 41
    4.3 Sadat's Motivations for Peace 43
    4.4 Peace with Israel 44
    4.5 Future of Normalization 45

5. Relations with the Arab World 47
    5.1 Perceptions of Egyptian Leadership 47
    5.2 Relations with the Saudis 47
    5.3 Egypt's Isolation 48
    5.4 A Low Point in Relations 48
    5.5 Steps Toward Reintegration 50
    5.6 Egypt's Diplomatic Role in the
        Iran-Iraq War 51
    5.7 Relations with Libya and the Sudan 52

6. Relations with the Superpowers 55
    6.1 Relations with the United States 55
    6.2 Relations with the Soviet Union 56
    6.3 The Danger of Alliance 58

7. Relations with Europe and the Third World 61
    7.1 The West 61
    7.2 China 61
    7.3 Third World Relations 62

8. Future Prospects
   8.1 Mubarak's Hold on Power   63
   8.2 Implications of the People's Assembly
       Elections   63
   8.3 Looming Problems   64
   8.4 Egyptian Sovereignty and the
       United States   65
   8.5 Islamic Fundamentalism   65
   8.6 Bureaucracy and Corruption   66
   8.7 The Danger of Rising Expectations   66
   8.8 Maintaining the Economic and Political
       Momentum   66
   8.9 The Economy   67
   8.10 The Balancing Act   68

III. Economic Analysis

1. Summary Conclusions   71
   1.1 Resources   71
   1.2 Recent Economic Developments   71
   1.3 Direction of Policy   71
   1.4 Macroeconomic Developments   71
   1.5 Sectoral Developments   71
   1.6 Balance of Payments   72
   1.7 Financial Sector   72

2. Macro-Economic Analysis   73
   2.1 Pre-Liberalization Economy   73
   2.2 The Open Door Policy   74
   2.3 State of the Economy: 1978-1983   76
   2.4 Effects of Liberalization: 1973-1983   77

3. Development Planning and Public Policy
   3.1 Current Development Strategy and
       Development Issues   81
   3.2 The 1982-1986 Plan   81
   3.3 Objectives of the Plan   82
   3.4 Human Resource Development Policy   83
   3.5 Industrial Sector   84
   3.6 Agricultural Sector   85
   3.7 Labor Migration Policies   86
   3.8 Recent Economic Policies   87
   3.9 Consequences of Recent Policies   88
   3.10 Emergency Reforms   90
   3.11 General Evaluation   90
   3.12 Technology   92
   3.13 Medium-term Prospects   92
   3.14 External Factors   93

4. Petroleum Sector
   4.1 Sector Growth 95
   4.2 Short-term Production Adjustments 96
   4.3 Natural Gas 97

5. Industry
   5.1 Sluggish Overall Growth 99
   5.2 Future Growth Dependent on Economic Reforms 99
   5.3 Reduced Labor Migration and Growing Population 100

6. Agricultural Sector 103
   6.1 Low Growth 103
   6.2 Policy Problems 103
   6.3 Technological Problems 104

7. Manpower 105
   7.1 Employment Effects on Liberalization 105
   7.2 Continuing Problem Areas 105
   7.3 Reduced Migration Creates New Problems 106

8. Construction Sector 109
   8.1 Role in Development Strategy 109
   8.2 Boom Taxing Capacity 109

9. Finance Sector 111
   9.1 Increasing Liquidity and High Inflation 111
   9.2 Measures to Stem Inflation 112
   9.3 Prospects for Public Finance 113
   9.4 Banks 113
   9.5 Increased Powers for the Central Bank 113
   9.6 Islamic Banking 114

10. Other Sectors of Importance 115
    10.1 Distribution and Service Sectors 115
    10.2 Tourism 115

11. Foreign Trade
    11.1 Overall Situation 117
    11.2 Source of Short-lived Current Strength 117
    11.3 Recent Estimates 118
    11.4 Prospects 119

12. Foreign Business Outlook 123
    12.1 Foreign Private Investment 123
    12.2 Impact of Liberalization 123
    12.3 Changes in Exchange System 124

12.4	Short-term Opportunities	124
12.5	Longer-term Caution	124
12.6	U.S. Investment Disappointing	125

IV. Statistical Appendix

Table 1.	Basic Information	129
Table 2.	Cabinet List	131
Table 3.	Political Parties	132
Table 4.	May 1984 Election Results	132

Defense

Table 5.	Egyptian Military Equipment and Personnel	134
Table 6.	Treaties in Effect: Egypt-USA	137
Table 7.	Trade in Major Conventional Weapons	138
Table 8.	Military Expenditure in Constant and Current Prices	140
Table 9.	Major Arms Suppliers, 1978-1982	140
Table 10.	Value of Arms Transfers	141
Table 11.	Military Expenditure: 1975-1982	141

Demography

Table 12.	Population Density in Major Urban Centers	144
Table 13.	Population, Rates of Birth, Death and Natural Increase	144
Table 14.	Population of Major Cities	145
Table 15.	Chief Demographic Indicators	145
Table 16.	Population by Governorate	146

Economy

Table 17.	Economic Indicators	148
Table 18.	Growth in Gross Domestic Product	148
Table 19.	Gross Domestic Product at Current Prices	149
Table 20.	Gross Domestic Product by Sector at Constant Prices	150

Banking and Finance

Table 21.	Financial Survey	152
Table 22.	Fiscal Summary	153

Table 23.	Factors Affecting Monetary Expansion	153
Table 24.	Summary of Fiscal Operations	154
Table 25.	Consumer Price Index for Urban Population	156
Table 26.	Distribution of Private Sector Credit	156
Table 27.	Interest Rate Survey	157
Table 28.	Lending Rates of Interest	157
Table 29.	Exchange Rates	158

Budget and Planning

Table 30.	Budget Outline	160
Table 31.	Functional Classification of Current Expenditure	161
Table 32.	Total Investment of the Five Year Plan by Public/Private Sector	162
Table 33.	Total Investment of the Five Year Plan by Economic Sector	163
Table 34.	Budget History	164
Table 35.	Proposed Industrial Investment	164

Debt

Table 36.	Debt Service on Medium and Long Term Debt	166
Table 37.	Structure of Outstanding External Obligations	168
Table 38.	Civilian Public Debt Service	170

Energy

Table 39.	Production and Distribution of Petroleum, Natural Gas and Petroleum Products	172
Table 40.	Production of Petroleum Products	172
Table 41.	Petroleum Production 1977-1983	173
Table 42.	Egyptian Oil and Gas Discoveries	174
Table 43.	Refinery Location, Ownership and Capacity	176
Table 44.	Energy Supply and Demand	176
Table 45.	Production, Consumption and Export of Petroleum Products	177
Table 46.	Crude Petroleum Exports by Source	178
Table 47.	Exports and Imports of Crude Petroleum Products	178
Table 48.	Petroleum Export Price	179

Industry

| Table 49. | Industrial Production | 182 |
| Table 50. | Subsidies Paid by Central Government | 183 |

Agriculture

Table 51.	Production of major Agricultural Crops	186
Table 52.	Indices of Agriculture Production and Yield	188
Table 53.	Supply and Demand for Major Agricultural Commodities	189
Table 54.	Trade Performance and Self-sufficiency for Principal Agricultural Commodities	190
Table 55.	Principal Crop Production	191
Table 56.	Meat and Poultry Production	191
Table 57.	Bilateral Agricultural Treaties in Effect: Egypt-USA	192
Table 58.	Livestock Population	193
Table 59.	Agricultural Sector Development	193

Trade

Table 60.	Balance of Payments	196
Table 61.	Balance of Payments Summary	197
Table 62.	Trade by Commodity Sections	197
Table 63.	Balance of Payments- Detailed Current Account	198
Table 64.	Balance of Payments- Detailed Capital Account	199
Table 65.	Main Commodities Traded	200
Table 66.	Main Trading Partners	201
Table 67.	Foreign Trade Indicators	202
Table 68.	Commodity Composition of Exports	202

Labor

| Table 69. | Employment by Economic Sector | 204 |
| Table 70. | Distribution of Employment | 205 |

Transportation and Communications

Table 71.	Tourist Activity	208
Table 72.	Infrastructure	208
Table 73.	Suez Canal Traffic and Revenues	208

Health, Education, and Welfare

Table 74.	Educational Enrollment	210
Table 75.	Public Expenditure on Education	211
Table 76.	Health Care Indicators	211

I. BACKGROUND

1. **GEOGRAPHY.** Egypt has a total land area of 1,101,449 sq km (1 sq km= 0.386 sq mi), of which 96.5 percent is desert, waste, or urban. Of the remaining surface area, only 2.8 percent is cultivated, while 0.7 percent is land water. The extremes of length and breadth are 1,080 km (1 km = 0.62 mi) and 1,232 km, respectively. Located in northeast Africa, Egypt is bordered by Israel and the Red Sea on the east, the Sudan on the south, Libya on the west, and the Mediterranean on the north. Of four geographical regions, the Nile River Valley (1,080 km long) and its Delta is the most important and is where the population is concentrated. Second in importance is the Sinai Peninsula, which is viewed by Egyptians as a geopolitical barrier to Israel and which is the site of most of Egypt's present oil production. The two other regions are the Western Desert (with sizeable oases which may possess considerable water resources) and the Eastern Highlands (slightly elevated and rugged terrain cut by deep valleys).

2. **CLIMATE.** The climate of Egypt is relatively uniform with two seasons, winter and summer. From November to April mean temperatures range from 8° C to 30° C (45° F and 85° F) while in the summer from May to October mean temperatures can range from 21° to 35° C (71° F and 96° F). Egypt has scant rainfall (200 mm/year). The temperature can fall considerably during the night, particularly in the desert regions. Humidity is fairly low, especially in inland areas.

3. **POPULATION.** At the present time, the population is estimated to be about 46 million, concentrated in the 3.5 percent of habitable land. Most of this population is crammed into the narrow Nile River Valley, resulting in one of the highest urban population densities in the world (2,800 per sq km). Slightly less than half (45.37 percent) of the population is urban.

The birth rate has tended to rise slightly in recent years, half-hearted attempts at birth control having proved largely unsuccessful. The death rate has fallen steadily, reflecting higher health standards. The rate of natural population increase seems to have stabilized around 3 percent. Annual growth rate for 1982 was 2.8 percent.

Emigration (nearly all of it economically motivated) has, however, affected the demographic situation. Some 1.7 million Egyptians are believed to be living abroad, mostly in wealthier Arab countries where they are profitably employed. The majority of these are not, however, permanent emigrants.

Sunni Muslims constitute an estimated 93 percent of the population. No other Muslim sect is officially recognized. The Christian community is dominated by the monophysite Copts, but there are small Catholic sects (of the Greek, Armenian and Syrian rites), Orthodox sects (of the Greek, and Armenian rites), and Protestant communities (mostly Coptic converts).

Egypt has a high degree of ethnic homogeneity — 96 percent — the only non-Arab minority of note being the Nubians, who constitute less than 1 percent of the population and are concentrated in the south. The number of foreign residents has diminished sharply since the post-revolutionary revocation of privileges accorded holders of foreign passports, but there are still a few Greeks, Italians and Maltese, living mostly in the cities. There are large numbers of Arabic-speaking Bedouins, with distinct customs and traditions and a nomadic way of life, inhabiting mostly the desert areas.

4. RESOURCES. The major source of agricultural water is the Nile River which, since the completion of the Aswan High Dam, provides for more reliable perennial irrigation. Anticipated expansion of usage in the 1980s may create conditions of scarcity. Seventy percent of the 2.8 percent cultivated land area is multiple cropped. The prospects for expanding the cultivated area are limited — 912,000 feddans were reclaimed between 1952 and 1975 (1 feddan = 1.038 acres).

Although oil was once a negligible factor in Egypt's economy, Egypt became marginally self-sufficient in oil in the 1970s. Under the Sinai II Agreement, Egypt regained the western portion of its oil fields, but did not become an exporter until after the Peace Treaty and total Israeli withdrawal. In 1983 production averaged 719,000 barrels/day, 11 percent more than in 1982 (649,000 b/d).

Proven reserves of this low-sulphur-content oil are estimated to be 3.1 billion barrels with a reserve life of 16.0 years at present production levels. Egypt's proven reserves of natural gas as of January 1981 were 84.96 billion cu m (3 trillion cu ft) and production was at the equivalent of 2,080.8 metric tons/day. In 1982/83 total natural gas production came to 2.2 million metric tons. With regard to other minerals, Egypt has virtual self-sufficiency in phosphates and possesses some iron deposits and potentially commercially exploitable deposits of uranium (with anticipated production of 30-50 tons annually).

5. SOCIAL STRUCTURE. Egyptian society is essentially elitist in character, with the military officers, techno-bureaucrats, landowners, and the religious establishment dominating the urban proletariat and unemployed and peasants. Although upper and middle class women now enjoy considerable rights and have entered the work force in substantial numbers, the overwhelming majority of women still have only second-class status. This is suggested by the enrollment figures for primary education (88 percent for males versus 56 percent for females).

6. RELIGION. Sunni Muslims constitute an overwhelming majority (some 93 percent) of the population. Coptic Christians are the most important other sect; they include many professionals and are usually guaranteed (unofficially) a few seats in the National Assembly and at least one cabinet post.

Since the late nineteenth century, Egypt has moved in the direction of increasing secularism. While Islam remained the official religion, some of Egypt's most celebrated national leaders (like Saad Zaghlul) distanced themselves from the Muslim clergy and had Christian associates. The trend was, however, reversed in recent years. As Sadat cracked down on most opposition groups, the only significant groups which remained immune were the religious right, whose influence grew disproportionately in the late 1970s spurred on by the growing antipathy to prevailing materialistic attitudes and a sense of confrontation with the west intensified by the Iranian revolution. Sadat sought to appease the Islamic fundamentalists by decreeing that the Sharia was the sole source of legislation in Egypt. He did not, however, succeed in containing them, and was assassinated by a self-professed Muslim fundamentalist.

The Coptic community, which has generally maintained friendly relations with the government, became more militant in response to the growing militancy of the Islamic movements, and also in response to repressive measures adopted by Sadat in an awkward attempt to placate the Islamic fundamentalists.

7. MILITARY The defense structure is headed by the president, the Supreme Commander, who appoints the four Chiefs of Staff. The armed forces consist of 447,000 men with 1,940 tanks and 500 combat aircraft.

The army comprises 315,000 men, (180,000 conscripts). The navy has 20,000 men (15,000 conscripts), and is generally of little importance. The air force (which boasts 27,000 men, 10,000 of whom are conscripts) has grown considerably in importance; the current president, Mubarak, rose from its ranks.

The military (the army in particular) has played a major political role since the revolution. Under Nasser, military officers enjoyed economic privileges, many of which they still retain. The relevance of the military to the political process was illustrated by their intervention to save the regime in 1977, and their quick action to restore order in the wake of the assassination of President Sadat.

Expenditure on defense has risen steadily despite the peace treaty with Israel. In 1983/84 it stood at $3.043 billion (compared to $2.495 billion in the previous fiscal year). Egypt attaches importance to diversifying its sources of weaponry, but the United States is currently the major supplier. The armed forces still use Soviet equipment (much of it outdated), for which spare parts are not easy to obtain.

The weaknesses of the Egyptian military include: political entanglement and a considerable degree of politicization (there is believed to be a significant cell of Islamic oppositionist officers), uneven quality of training, lack of coordination of weapons systems, and an inadequate reserve system.

Egypt has military treaty obligations to various Arab states, although these have been technically superseded by the Camp David agreement. Egypt has supplied weapons and spare parts to Iraq in the latter's war with Iran, and generally maintains a growing export industry in locally manufactured arms. Facilities are accorded U.S. troops in Egypt, but no formal agreement guarantees continued access to these facilities.

8. ECONOMIC STRUCTURE. The economy is dominated by the public sector, but in recent years the Open Door Policy has encouraged the expansion of the private sector. The 1980-1984 Five-Year Plan focuses on a 10 percent increase in the Gross Domestic Product. Priority is given to agricultural projects and agro-industries. Industrialization of the building sector and the construction industry are also high on the priority list. The economy is basically agricultural. Agriculture constitutes about 25 percent of the GDP and engages 40-50 percent of the labor force of 12 million. The industrial sector (excluding petroleum) accounts for 17 percent of the GDP and 13 percent of total employment. In 1980 and 1981, the economy registered 8 percent in real growth; in 1982 the economy showed 5.3 percent in real growth. The balance of payments improved significantly with a drop in the deficit from $3 billion in 1975 to $600 million surplus in 1980. This favorable trend, however, has reversed, with the 1982 balance of payments in deficit at slightly more than $1.4 billion and the 1983/84 deficit projected at $2.5 billion. This is almost entirely the result of public sector deficit spending. In 1982/83, the major sources of revenue included: petroleum sales of $2.7 billion, remittances from expatriate workers of $3.1 billion, Suez Canal revenues ot over $600 million and earnings from tourism of $600 million.

9. INFRASTRUCTURE. Radio programs are broadcast over 27 medium-wave (domestic) and 16 short-wave (international) transmitters for a weekly total of 1,200 broadcast hours. In 1982, there were 6.5 million radios. Television broadcasts began in 1960. The number of television sets in 1982 was estimated at 1.9 million (40 per 1,000).

Beginning in 1875 with the premier daily al-Ahram, Egypt has had a sustained history of quality journalism. Al-Ahram's daily circulation of 400,000 combines with that of the more mass-oriented al-Akhbar's figure of 650,000 to dominate the field of seventeen major daily newspapers and a total daily circulation of approximately 3 million. Daily newspapers include some issued by the opposition parties, although these are periodically banned. There is a total of 25 non-dailies and 38 periodicals.

The telephone system has deteriorated in quality in recent years. The 1980 agreement with Siemens of West Germany and Austria plus Thomson C.S.F. of France to begin a $1.8 billion modernization program holds promise for correcting the problems of supply and reliability. Long distance service has already improved through the use of microwave. There were a total of 532,021 telephones in use in January of 1981; the figure was expected to rise to 775,000 in 1982.

Twelve thousand kilometers of paved roads (43 percent of the total) and 15,000 km of unpaved roads carry 80 percent of the freight tonnage. Egyptian Railways has 4,882 km of railway in standard gauge (1,435 mm) with 2,327 km of auxiliary lines. The 1970s saw a decrease in rail usage due to equipment shortages. Besides the major inland waterway of the Nile River and its canal system (local capacities of 200 to 920 tons), the Suez Canal is the major canal of the country. It is 163 km long and has been widened and deepened to handle 150,000 dwt ships with a draft of 53 feet. Revenues in 1983 amounted to $970.1 million, as 22,224 ships with a net tonnage of 578,226,000 passed through the canal. The SUMED oil pipeline went into operation in 1976 and is able to transport 80 million tons of crude annually from Ain Sokhna on the Red Sea to near Alexandria on the Mediterranean. Egypt Air possesses 11 aircraft and in 1977 carried 959,000 passengers. Passengers carried during the late 1970s increased at an annual rate of about 16 percent; nearly 80 percent of domestic passengers were foreign tourists.

Total electricity production in 1982 was approximately 19 billion kwh. The installed capacity in 1980 was 3,200 mw; of that total 2,500 mw came from the High Dam and Aswan Dam.

10. SOCIAL SERVICES. The national literacy rate in 1981 was 44 percent. During 1978/79, there were 4,287,124 students enrolled in primary schools, 929,262 in secondary schools, and 443,696 in eleven universities. There were 127,021 primary teachers and a total of 106,265 other teachers from secondary to university education. Egypt spends about 7 percent of GNP on education (1979). In addition, the high rate of population increase requires increasing expenditures on new buildings. Each governorate prepares its own budget and submits this to the Ministry of Education in the cabinet, which then must approve it. Final budgets are ratified by the National Assembly.

Egypt's health care system is improving. In 1980, population per physician was 970 and life expectancy was 55 for males and 58 for females.

II. POLITICAL ANALYSIS

1.
SUMMARY CONCLUSIONS

1.1 THE PRESIDENT. Mubarak's transition to the presidency has proven to be smooth. He has proved himself an effective operator in Egypt's political environment although he cannot act in the free-wheeling, self-assured style of his predecessor. His greatest problem — which he will find increasingly challenging — is to overcome his do-nothing image. The national inclination of Egyptians to look for a strong — not necessarily dramatic — leadership figure will work to Mubarak's advantage. Although his honesty, sincerity, and integrity are not questioned, growing numbers of Egyptians are concluding that he may not be capable of formulating or implementing policies which can benefit the majority of the population. His recent handling of the national elections in May 1984 improved his image somewhat.

1.2 THE GOVERNMENT. Egypt is not a pure parliamentary democracy. Because of the National Democratic Party's overwhelming majority, a government defeat on any issue of importance is unthinkable. Nevertheless, the People's Assembly is not a mere rubber-stamp. Individual members can and do sharply criticize the government and call for investigations and official replies to specific charges. Criticism of the government and its officials is becoming an increasingly important factor in policy decisions. Mubarak appears to want greater political liberalization for Egypt, but his concept of democracy falls considerably short of the western model. Feedback from moderate opponents is an important element of his leadership style, but he places a high priority on maintaining control. Mubarak's difficult relations with the opposition indicate that he is ambivalent about political reform. He is likely to continue his slow evolution toward democracy — particularly if he believes this is a way of leaving his mark on Egyptian history — but an unruly People's Assembly could lead him to withdraw some of the newly granted political freedoms.

1.3 THREATS TO STABILITY. Political life in Egypt is remarkably stable. Attempts by the domestic opposition or outsiders to incite discontent have made little headway. Economic distress and issues concerning Egypt's sovereignty over its own territories seem to be the only problems with the potential to generate widespread instability. However, the government will face a challenge from the appeal of fundamentalist Islam if it does not come to grips with the underlying frustrations on which radicalism and violence feed. There is no immediate threat to stability from the turn toward fundamentalism in general or from extremist Islamic groups in particular.

1.4 THE OPPOSITION. The opposition is fragmented and lacks dynamic leadership. The power structure of the Islamic establishment is diffuse, a condition which affords the government an impressive degree of control over it. The left has considerable organizational talent, but has only limited appeal for the generally conservative population. The illegal communist movement is small and weak. As a result of mutual suspicions and ideological incompatibilities, neither the right nor the left has been able to present a united front.

1.5 THE MILITARY. The Egyptian military — specifically its lower grade officers and the rank and file — is a microcosm of Egyptian society and is not an elite organization. It is affected by the same economic and social problems which afflict the society as a whole. Thus far, the higher echelons have been content to stand behind Mubarak. Should this support be withdrawn Mubarak would become highly vulnerable politically.

1.6 THE ECONOMY. Built-in distortions in the economy seriously limit the government's ability to resolve the problems which frustrate most Egyptians. The structural reforms needed to advance Egypt's economic recovery and to promote long-term growth necessarily foster discontent and political unrest. As a result, the economy is geared toward satisfying consumer demand and contributing to short-term stability.

1.7 RELATIONS WITH ISRAEL. Israel's invasion of Lebanon, viewed in the context of other unilateral actions taken by Israel since the signing of the 1978 Camp David Framework for Peace, underscores Egypt's frustration and diplomatic impotence in affecting Israel's behavior in the interests of comprehensive peace. The cumulative effect of Israel's actions has caused Egyptians to question the Israeli government's commitment to the principle of exchanging territory for peace. In increasing numbers, Egyptians are asking whether Begin negotiated the 1979 peace treaty as a first step toward establishing peace with all of Israel's neighbors, or whether he intended to "neutralize" Egypt in order to free resources for the expansion and consolidation of "greater Israel." Few, if any, Egyptians retain hope that progress toward peace and a genuine improvement in Egyptian-Israeli relations are possible.

1.8 RELATIONS WITH THE ARABS. Egypt's contacts with other Arab leaders have increased considerably since Mubarak took power. Eventual rapprochement is inevitable, but the process is likely to be gradual and vulnerable to events in the region. Since the Mubarak-Arafat talks, Mubarak's criticism of United States and Israeli actions in Lebanon as well as his public disapproval of the expanded U.S.-Israeli strategic relationship have brought the Egyptian posture into closer alignment with the Arab camp. Jordan led the way by re-establishing diplomatic relations with Cairo on September 25, 1984.

1.9 RELATIONS WITH THE SOVIETS. Limited improvement in Egypt's relations with the Soviet Union seems probable. Sadat's personal antipathy toward Moscow was central in reducing Egyptian-Soviet relations to an all-time low. The new leadership has not expressed a similarly deep-seated hostility and Mubarak was not directly associated with the antagonistic actions Sadat took against the Soviets. In fact, in the summer of 1984 Egypt announced that it would resume diplomatic relations with the Soviet Union at the ambassadorial level, but this will not signal a fundamental shift in Egyptian policy.

1.10 RELATIONS WITH THE UNITED STATES. The relationship between Egypt and the United States is generally excellent. There are tensions, however, which result from differences in national interests in several areas — particularly as regards U.S. policies toward Israel and regional strategy — and from different perceptions of how those interests can best be served. The newly strengthened strategic relationship between Israel and the

United States is the freshest source of tension. Senior grade Egyptian officers fear the Israeli regime will be encouraged to adventurism; political analysts fear the arrangement will make the Israelis more intransigent on Lebanese withdrawal and West Bank settlements. All complain that American election year politics removes any incentive for Israel to compromise.

1.11 REGIONAL SECURITY ISSUES. Egyptians have mixed feelings about America's increased interest in regional security. Most Egyptians welcome U.S. military assistance, but are sensitive about "bases" and foreign military influence.

2. POLITICAL STRUCTURE

2.1 POLITICAL INSTITUTIONS. The present political structure in Egypt was established by Sadat in 1971. Egypt has a republican form of government with executive powers concentrated in the presidency. Under the 1971 Constitution, the president is nominated by a one-third vote of the People's Assembly, with approval by a two-thirds vote of the same body, and elected by popular referendum.

The People's Assembly is composed of 448 delegates. Seats in the Assembly are allocated by party according to the share of the vote each party gets in each election district. Only parties that receive at least 8 percent of the vote nationwide are represented in the Assembly. Seats remaining after proportional distribution go to the party with the most votes nationwide. Delegates serve five-year terms. Under the Constitution, the president can dissolve the Assembly at any time, but this action must be approved by popular referendum and a new election held within 60 days.

The People's Assembly has important constitutional powers, in addition to the nomination of the president. It shares with the president the authority to propose legislation and approves the government's general policy and budget. Assembly deputies have the right to question ministers, the prime minister, and even the president. The Assembly also has the power to pass a vote of no confidence in any cabinet minister.

In practice, however, the People's Assembly has exercised few of its constitutional powers. It is primarily a forum for public debate, channeling public grievances to government agencies, and recommending solutions for areas of government failure. It routinely ratifies decisons made by the president and the government — a pattern set during the early part of Nasser's rule, when Sadat was the Speaker of the Assembly. Only the Assembly's budget committee has been active and fairly effective in recent years in influencing budget policy.

The Shura Council (Consultative Council), created by Sadat in 1980, is Egypt's other parliamentary institution.

It is an advisory body and has no legislative powers. The Council has 140 elected members who serve six-year terms, and 70 members appointed by the president. Elections for half of the Council's seats are held every three years. The party that gets a simple majority of the votes wins all the seats in the Council.

The changes in the constitution that were approved by referendum in 1980 made it possible for the president to be reelected indefinitely (instead of for two terms only), made the Sharia (Islamic religious law) the source of law, and gave constitutional status to the multi-party system.

2.2 LEADERSHIP. The nature of Egyptian leadership today remains much as it has been in the past: authority-centered, hierarchical, rooted in tradition. These elements, so apparent at the national level, are replicated in the family, in the village, at school, and in the workplace. Whatever ideology may be used to put a public face on the current ruling power, these elements in fact pre-date Islam. They are reinforced by Muslim values and political ideology, transmitted to modern Egypt through the Ottomans and their predecessors and interpreted and supported by the religious authorities.

Centralized power from Cairo dominates Egyptian patterns of leadership from the village umda (headman) to the mayor of the principal city of the district, to the governor of the province, to the cabinet minister(s) in Cairo responsible for local government functions, to the rectors of the national universities who hold ministerial rank, to the officer corps of the military and the gendarmerie — all draw their authority from the legislature and ultimately the president. Indeed, the legislature itself is dominated by the presidency.

After the military brought off the 1952 revolution, the nation's leadership was drawn largely from among the ranks of the officer corps. Indeed, it could be said that the officer corps of the Egyptian military came to replace the old pasha class in privilege and power. Under President Nasser, the chief positions of government at both the local and national levels were filled in overwhelming numbers by military officers. Although this trend was partially attenuated by President Sadat after 1973, leadership by the military has tended to bolster and maintain the traditional, authoritarian nature of Egyptian leadership.

Nevertheless, despite this basic authoritarian structure, few Egyptian leaders have ever been able to exercise absolute power, and Egyptians have always found ways to express opposition or innovation — be it through writing, through humor, or, not infrequently, through demonstrations and rebellion. Political power is centralized and authoritarian, but rule is seldom successful in Egypt without consent and legitimacy. Furthermore, Egyptian leaders themselves have been an integral part of the changes in Egyptian society. While there remains a strong streak of paternalism, the leaders on the whole are becoming more enlightened, better educated, more liberal minded, and more comfortable with the institutions of representative government — a legislature, an independent judiciary, opposition parties, and limited freedom of the press.

However, the link between leadership and the military remains firm. No Egyptian can remain president without the support of the military. Change is coming only slowly; under serious challange, the leadership would almost certainly revert to its basic authoritarian pattern. Nonetheless, there is movement. President Mubarak, who last May presided over the first genuinely free elections in Egypt since before 1952, may represent the beginning of a transition toward a less authority-oriented leadership.

2.3 THE MILITARY. The role of the military in Egypt has undergone continuous evolution from the time of the Free Officers' seizure of power in 1952.

In the first decade following the Revolution, members of the Free Officers Organization and their supporters in the army moved into commanding positions in government, civil administration, and economic management. Military men were placed in second and third level echelons as well as in top posts. At the same time President Nasser carried out a large-scale expansion of the armed forces, prompted in part by the growing military prowess of neighboring Israel, by Israeli actions against Egypt, and by the formation of the western-aligned Baghdad Pact. These external challenges enhanced the army's importance and prestige and reinforced the militarization of Egyptian politics. Not only was the army the vehicle of the Revolution, but it was viewed as the defender of the nation in time of peril.

Politicization. The politicization of the military eventually contributed to a loss of military prestige. Loyalty to the regime became a more important criterion for promotion than competence. The consequences of this policy, first evidenced by the poor performance of Egyptian forces in the Yemeni war, were made devastatingly clear by the June 1967 war with Israel. This debacle discredited the army in the eyes of the Egyptian populace, and created a sentiment within the military itself for a more professional, non-political, officer corps.

Anwar Sadat, who became president in 1970, reduced the role of the military in Egyptian politics. He appointed an unprecedented number of non-military men to top posts, but insured the military's loyalty by the appointment of Hosni Mubarak, the commander of Egypt's air force in 1973, as vice president and by the acquisition of advanced weaponry from the United States. Renewal of limited civilian political activity under President Mubarak is likely to further diminish the role of the Egyptian military in politics.

Sadat's assassination by a military-religious cell notwithstanding, it is likely that the army leadership and second-rank officers will play a diminishing political role. This trend will be reversed only in case of renewed hostilities with Israel, or major civil unrest in which the army would be called upon to restore and maintain order.

The Military Structure. The defense structure is headed by the president, who is the Supreme Commander and who appoints the four Chiefs of Staff. The armed forces consist of 447,000 men: 315,000 in the army, approximately 20,000 in the navy and almost 100,000 in the air force and air defense command combined.

Although the military in Egypt has a record of obedience and loyalty to the nation's political leaders, information on the attitudes of armed forces personnel, particularly field grade officers, is sketchy. The extent of Mubarak's popularity with the Egyptian military is unclear, but there has been no evidence of widespread dissension. Minister of Defense Abu Ghazala appears to be personally, professionally, and politically loyal to the president. In autumn 1983, Mubarak shifted assignments among the senior officer corps, placing officers close to him in positions of greater influence. This move strengthened Mubarak's position with the military at least marginally, and gave a signal to any who doubted that the president is the boss.

Most officers seem to support peace with Israel and the evolving military relationship with the United States. The military's view of Mubarak will be influenced by his success in satisfying the armed forces' need for new equipment. Already there are some who criticize U.S. military assistance as too little and too late, and who draw unfavorable comparisons between U.S. support and that provided earlier by the Soviet Union.

2.4 RELIGIOUS AFFAIRS. Two themes characterize modern Egyptian history. The first is a shared destiny with other Muslim Arabs which provides substance for pan-Arab ambitions. The second is Egypt's early initiation into the modern nation-state system, to which it was introduced in the first half of the nineteenth century by Mohammed Ali. From that point onward, Islam in Egypt, both as a doctrine and as a social institution, repeatedly has been challenged by foreign political dominance, western science and technology, and alien social theories.

In dealing with the problems of rapid modernization, two basic societal assets have been helpful. First, Egyptian society is remarkably homogeneous, with 90 percent of the population Sunni Muslims — Islam's historic ruling majority. Second, traditionally, Egyptians have been a settled people living either in large urban centers or residing in the narrow band of the Nile River and Delta.

Structure of Islamic Authority. Egypt has no hierarchical religious structure which would enable a paramount religious figure to issue instructions that would be reflected in Friday sermons throughout the land. Instead, power is distributed among five entities: the Shaikh of al-Azhar, the Mufti, the Ministry of Religious Endowments, the Muslim Brotherhood, and the Sufi sects. The first three belong to the legal establishment. The Muslim Brotherhood is illegal but often officially tolerated. The Sufi sects, once a potent force in Egyptian village life linking the rural areas together, are legal but not always tolerated.

- **The Shaikh of al-Azhar.** Al-Azhar University is regarded by most Sunni Muslims as the intellectual center of Islam. Its Sheikh or Rector possesses substantial authority in principle, but in fact lacks independence and power to use his authority effectively. The chief of state appoints the Sheikh from among a 50-member council of ulema connected with the University. However, it is to the Sheikh and the ulema around him that most, though not all, Muslim leaders in Egypt (imams) look for moral and political guidance. The Sheikh shapes opinion through his public statements, private persuasion, and influence over groups such as the Muslim Brotherhood. He exercises more direct control over Friday sermons in mosques owned by al-Azhar.

- **The Mufti.** As the nation's highest authority on Islamic law, the Mufti has responsibility for determining whether national legislation is consistent with the Sharia (Islamic law). In practice, his duties are ceremonial: he makes pronouncements on religious matters (after consultation with the government and the Shaikh of al-Azhar), he announces the sighting of the moon for religious festivals, he confirms death sentences passed by the courts. The Mufti is a religious scholar appointed by the government. The Mufti contributes to the diffuseness of religious authority by withholding from more powerful centers the right to declare legislation inconsistent with Islamic law.

— **The Ministry of Religious Endowments.** Religious endowments (waqf, pl. awqaf), a considerable traditional source of revenue and power, were nationalized by Nasser after the 1952 Revolution. Through the ministry's Department of Sermons and Guidance, the government exercises authority over many of Egypt's imams. The imams of government-owned mosques are paid by the government and are in effect civil servants. The Ministry sends them periodic guidance for their sermons.

— **The Muslim Brotherhood.** The Muslim Brotherhood, founded in 1928 in Egypt from whence it spread throughout the Arab world, is the oldest Islamic fundamentalist political organization in the Middle East. The organization's ideological legacy remains a significant force in North Africa and in Syria, Jordan, and Saudi Arabia. The Brotherhood's basic call is for an "Islamic order," a set of moral or ethical principles which serve as guidelines. In practical terms, this means substituting the Islamic Sharia for western-inspired legal systems, basing the economy on Quranic principles, and encouraging women to remain in the home. The Brotherhood's appeal is mainly to the marginally employed urban lower middle classes — government clerks, civil servants, students — for whom the ideology of the Brotherhood offers an attractive alternative to either communism or western-style capitalism. In Egypt, the Brotherhood has been alternately tolerated and ruthlessly suppressed, but remains a significant political force.

— **The Sufi Sects.** The sufi orders (<u>tariqas</u>), popular sects with greater or lesser degrees of mystical tendency, are a deeply rooted part of the religious scene in Egypt. Often inspired by a saint, the orders exercise both social and political influence at the local level, serving as a spiritual bulwark against the alien impact of secularism on the lower and middle classes. Presidents Nasser and Sadat maintained firm control of the orders – backed by the Azharis who view them as competitors – and tried to use the sects to make their policies acceptable. Since the assassination of Sadat, the sufi orders are keeping a low profile to avoid the appearance of collusion with religious extremism. However, clandestine connection between some of the tariqas and the Muslim Brotherhood is suspected, and President Mubarak is keeping a close watch on them. Given their long-term organization and traditional influence with the masses, the sufi orders continue to possess significant political potential both in rural villages and in congested urban quarters.

Resurgent Islam. The turn to religion in Egypt does not represent a unified resurgence, but rather a general mood stemming from societal stress and reinforced by the triumph of the Iranian revolution against the secularism of the Shah. Modernization has brought psychological and social displacements to Egypt, while failing to offer adequate substitutes for the Islamic ethical guides to equality and justice. People feel increasingly insecure as the traditional base for their personal, social, and moral identities erodes. In that void, Islam offers an enduring element of identity in a rapidly changing environment.

A decade of violent clashes between militant Islamic groups and government forces began in April 1974 with the seizure of a military academy in Cairo. Various groups subsequently carried out similar attacks, including the 1977 kidnapping and murder of a former cabinet minister and the assassination of President Sadat on October 6, 1981 by Takfir wa al-Hijra (Repentence and Emigration). Takfir and youth groups such as al-Jihad (Holy War) rose in the late 1960s, especially after the defeat in the 1967 war with Israel and the domestic failure to permit expression of dissenting views. The groups attracted educated Egyptians mostly from the rural areas and small towns. They demanded radical rejection of secular politics and return to Quranic social practices. They accepted violence as a means to attain their goals.

Mubarak's moves toward gradual democratization and freer expression of views have reduced the appeal of these groups. The government campaign against corruption has deprived religious extremists of justification for violent opposition to the regime.

The Copts. The only significant religious minority in Egypt, the Copts have been a source of intercommunal tension for centuries. Numbering between five and six million in a population of some forty-five million, the Copts are scattered around the country, with the largest concentration in rural upper Egypt. Despite Coptic protestations to the contrary, the government stresses its commitment to communal peace and does not deliberately discriminate against Copts. Fundamentalist Islamic organizations, however, do.

Outbreaks of religious strife between fundamentalists and Copts have been controlled by government security forces. The June 1981 intercommunal incidents in Cairo were the most serious in terms of the number of persons killed (14) and injured (75) since the January 1977 food riots. The head of the Coptic Orthodox Church, Pope Shenouda III and a number of his bishops were detained by Sadat in September 1981. Some of the bishops and clergy were subsequently released, but the government continues to withhold recognition of Shenouda as head of the church and community and confines him to quasi-isolation in a desert monastery. The arrest of Coptic leaders was in part a counterweight to the simultaneous arrest of Muslim religious figures, and in part a response to Shenouda's criticism of Sadat.

Copts express concern over the growth Islamic fundamentalism and fear a worsening of intercommunal tensions, but most observers agree there is less religious strife in Egypt in 1984 than in 1981.

2.5 SOCIAL STRUCTURE. The July Revolution of 1952 radically altered the structure of Egyptian society. The domination by large feudal landlords (often of Turkish or Circassian descent) was brought to an end by the Agrarian Reform Law which broke up large landholdings and distributed land to peasants. The nationalization program which followed put an end to the domination of the commercial establishment by a small number of families (many of them of Greek or Levantine origin) and set up a massive public sector staffed entirely by educated Egyptians.

The society that emerged had two salient features: the creation (through free and compulsory education) of an Egyptian intellectual elite with middle class aspirations, and the predominant role of the officer corps as the new privileged class. By the late sixties, it became clear that the inefficient and overstaffed public sector had failed to satisfy the aspirations of the middle class. The stunning military defeat in 1967 challenged the very raison d'etre of the military-dominated establishment. A measure of legitimacy was restored by the impressive performance of the armed forces in the 1973 war, but the pressure for change remained acute as heavy war costs debilitated the economy. It was in that context that Sadat embarked on his Open Door Policy (infitah).

Entrepreneurs. Sadat's measures insured the supremacy of the rising entrepreneurial class, which eclipsed the previously dominant officer and civil-servant classes. While the myth of a meritocracy was exploded, the Open Door Policy, coupled with the temporary opportunities of imigration to oil-rich Arab countries, gave the illusion of greater upward mobility. In fact, a relatively small number could become rich. The high inflation that accompanied the Open Door Policy, in tandem with the near-collapse of public services necessitating payment for what was once free, meant that many people were worse off than they had been.

While many basic necessities (e.g. housing, food) became considerably more expensive, the nouveau riche displayed no compunction about acquiring and flaunting various status symbols. Class differences thus also became more visible. The lot of the underprivileged (the peasants and the urban poor whose ranks were swelled by mass imigration from the countryside) deteriorated steadily. Peasants were penalized by a food subsidy that depressed the price of their produce. The urban poor either found no employment or took marginal jobs which netted them negligible income. Inflation eroded their earnings, and the housing shortage compelled them to make their homes in the streets or public cemeteries. Meanwhile, demand for consumer goods by the new rich far outstripped the productive capacity of the economy.

The restructuring of society was accompanied by a breakdown in social values. Honest hard work was no longer perceived as a prerequisite for success. Solidarity within families, and the traditional village ties which had provided the ultimate "safety net," were compromised by the cult of conspicuous consumption. Parasitism, laxity and outright dishonesty were tolerated by many as survival mechanisms in an age of increasing economic pressures.

Religious Reaction. The bitterness felt by the deprived classes was at least partly responsible for the resurgence of religion — which involved both Muslims and

Christians in Egypt. To many, the reaffirmation of spiritual beliefs was an appropriate response to growing materialism. As that materialism was associated with the Open Door Policy, it became convenient to label it as "alien" — or western.

The success of religious reaction in Egypt should not obscure a number of significant social factors. First, a socialist response to the capitalist ideology of the new elite would not necessarily have been any less valid to the masses than a religious one. Both would seem a natural reaction to the individualism, sybaritism and corruption that characterize the current system.

Second, economic conditions remain a major determinant of social phenomena. For example, economic pressures, rather than legal or political pressures, prompted women to seek employment in Nasser's Egypt. This phenomenon continues, religious conservatism notwithstanding.

Third, the Islamic resurgence reverses the trend toward secularism that began in Egypt as far back as Muhammad Ali in the early nineteenth century. Whatever else may be said about secularism in Egypt, it made possible the definition of a national identity along modern lines, in such a way that non-Muslim minorities did not feel excluded from the national ethos. It also engendered a drive toward material progress; the crude materialism of today is merely a mutation of that drive, by no means a necessary or irreversible one.

2.6 FACTORS FOR STABILITY AND INSTABILITY. The major factors which keep Egyptian society on a relatively even keel for the present are:

- a fairly strong leadership firmly supported by the Military, and to a lesser but sufficient degree by other key elements of society such as the business and professional community, the intellectuals, and the rural leadership;
- the success of the May elections, which denies extremists issues and a constituency;
- the basic conservative character of Egyptian society and the remarkable (but not bottomless) capacity of the individual Egyptian citizen to tolerate frustration and hardship;
- a relatively successful foreign policy that has yielded respect, support from the western powers, peace with Israel, and large amounts of military and economic aid from the United States, which insures continued military support for the president and mitigates the worst economic problems.

However, there are serious destabilizing forces within Egypt which could overwhelm the country and ramify negatively throughout the region if the delicate balance of stabilizing factors is upset.

- Chief among Egypt's problems is overpopulation — a net gain of one million people every ten months — with all the concommitant, cross-cutting problems;
- An urgent need exists for structural reforms in Egypt's economy The political and social dangers in such reforms could easily touch off widespread disorder.
- A growing, but still ungalvanized process of radicalization continues among religious and youth groups frustrated by Egypt's chronic economic problems — an anger that takes xenophobic, anti-western and anti-Israeli expressions.
- An increasingly visible gap between the rich and poor exists. This factor could provide the catalyst to fuse the disparate groups with various grievances against the government, especially if a leader emerged who provided charisma and a unifying message.

3.
INTERNAL DEVELOPMENTS

3.1 THE NASSER YEARS. The young officer's coup, which brought Gamal Abdel Nasser to power in Egypt in 1952, put an effective end to a dynasty and power structure that had prevailed in Egypt for a century and a half. The last scion of the Turkish-Albanian dynasty, King Farouk, was politely invited to depart via yacht for the life of a playboy dilettante in Europe. The old Turko-Arab landed aristocracy that had formed the ruling oligarchy found itself divested of power and of most of its lands. The drain of brains and of money abroad was a significant feature of the Nasser years in Egypt, especially after the land and commercial reform measures of the latter fifties.

Although bloodless, the 1952 Revolution was a true revolution. It shifted the base of real power from the monarchy/aristocracy to the military, especially the lower-middle-class, upwardly-mobile graduates of the military academies who constituted the cadre of professional officers. The Nasser government maintained the parliamentary structure of the previous era, but real power flowed from the officer's baton, not the ballot box. The issues that provoked the revolution were more pragmatic (corruption, waste, poverty) than ideological. Indeed, Nasser's efforts at formulating a theory ("Philosophy of the Revolution") and structure (the Arab Socialist Union) for his movement were explicitly cast in terms of the Pirandellesque "players in search of a playwright."

The domestic objectives of the Nasser regime were reformist and social. Primary goals of the period included land reform, universal education, and health care for the rural poor. Significant strides were made in each of these areas. Economic development was largely in the hands of the public sector, which expanded dramatically, but this was as much a result of necessity as of socialist doctrine. Only the public sector had the resources for the steel mills and other large prestige projects that were desired. Whatever its ultimate impact may turn out to be, the building of the Aswan High Dam truly captured the developmental spirit of the Nasser period in Egypt.

In the international arena, Nasser saw himself and his country as the center of a set of concentric circles encompassing the Arab World, Africa, and the Third World. Egypt was the most populous, the most powerful, and the most developed of all the countries in the Arab World, and after World War II became the seat of the Arab League. Egypt was also one of the most populous and developed countries in Africa, and assumed a role of growing leadership among the emerging nations of that continent. Nasser, especially after his masterful political handling of the Suez crisis of 1956, became (along with Nehru and Tito) one of the acknowledged leaders of the non-aligned nations. For the first fifteen years of his tenure, Nasser displayed considerable skill at juggling the great powers, balancing them against each other so as to achieve his own policy goals while maintaining a modicum of independence. American wheat and agricultural aid was set against Czech arms, Russian hydroelectric engineers jostled German missile experts, until the increasingly anti-Arab tilt of American policy in the mid-sixties pushed Nasser off his fulcrum.

The decline of Nasser actually began with the breakup of the United Arab Republic (the union of Egypt, Syria, and ultimately Yemen), from which Syria withdrew in 1961. The cream of Egypt's army was bogged down in the Yemeni civil war when Israel launched its second invasion of Sinai in 1967. Nasser's acrimonious rivalry with other Arab leaders contributed much to the Arab disarray that made Israel's 1967 conquests easy. At the same time, due in part to the population explosion, Nasser's domestic development programs were falling far short of the expectations they had raised. Resultant opposition was put down through increasingly repressive measures by the omnipresent security police, under which communists and Muslim Brothers suffered alike.

Nonetheless, Nasser's resignation after the 1967 war was withdrawn by popular demand and his death in 1970 left a gaping void in the hearts of his people. The spontaneous emotional outpouring of grief at Nasser's funeral stands in stark contrast to the very cool, correct tribute accorded his slain successor a decade later. For all his faults, Nasser was the father of modern Egypt.

3.2 TRANSITION TO SADAT. When Anwar Sadat became president in October 1970, he inherited a government that had been shaped by the personality of Gamal Abdel Nasser during his 16 years as Egypt's leader. The government and party apparatus reflected Nasser's thinking and style; it was composed of persons installed by him and loyal to him. Sadat, in the early months of his rule, was preoccupied with shoring up his position and could not effect even minor changes.

But changes in the style of governing were quickly apparent. Nasser's unquestioned control over the government and party had been a function of the many roles he played – president, prime minister, commander-in-chief of the armed forces, and head of Egypt's sole legal political organization, the Arab Socialist Union. After his death, these responsibilities were parceled out to the fallen leader's principal heirs. No individual was able to speak with Nasser's authority. Rule by uneasy consensus emerged.

This collegial arrangement, however, was short-lived. The "conspiracy" of April-May 1971 to overthrow Sadat resulted in the purge of virtually all those with whom Sadat, by force of circumstance, had been sharing power. Although persuasive evidence of an attempted coup has never been produced, there apparently was a move to restrict Sadat's growing tendency toward unilateral decisions and to reaffirm the principle of collegial rule. This challenge was thwarted.

Those implicated in the alleged plot included several of the most powerful members of the government, the Arab Socialist Union, and the public media. They were arrested and tried; many were sentenced to prison terms. Sadat, using the event as an opportunity to assert his control, proceeded with an ambitious restructuring of the government and party apparatus under the banner of eliminating "centers of power." Collectively, these changes marked the beginning of the de-Nasserization of Egypt.

The October 1973 war produced a rekindling of Egyptian political will. The Egyptian crossing of the Suez Canal and the initial reverses suffered by the Israeli army quickly erased the memory of the 1967 debacle. National pride and self-confidence were restored. One immediate effect of the war was that it made Sadat a charismatic leader and gave him a sense of authority and legitimacy which, in comparison to Nasser, he had seemed to lack.

3.3 SADAT TAKES CONTROL. Instead of using the war as an opportunity to further the revolution, Sadat turned to economic and political liberalization and the opening to the west. He began to stress the importance of revitalizing the Egyptian economy and set two basic economic goals. Like his predecessor, he hoped to push economic growth well ahead of population growth. He was equally determined to free Egypt from dependence on foreign largess, particularly reliance on the Soviet Union for arms. But the nationalization of private firms, haphazard implementation of economic plans, and improvident financial policies of Nasser's administration had created an import-dependent socialist economy unable either to earn or to borrow the massive amounts of foreign exchange required to accelerate growth.

The need to attract foreign economic assistance, both investment and aid, led to the introduction of <u>infitah</u> or the Open Door Policy. This need for foreign funds also necessitated the overhaul of Egypt's political structure — in part to convince foreign investors that the revolutionary politics and anti-capitalist ideology of Nasser's time were a thing of the past, and in part to demonstrate that Sadat and his government had a political legitimacy which, it was hoped, would lead to growing international economic confidence in Egypt.

Sadat also reasoned that as long as the Israelis occupied Egyptian territory, Egypt faced recurrent wars, costly in money and lives. Keeping Egypt's military machine ready for war consumed resources badly needed for the country's development and forced a reliance on foreign donors. But even then, Egypt was not strong enough to recover its lost territory by force of arms. Only negotiations held any promise of success, preferably negotiations in which the United States used its leverage over Israel to Egypt's benefit. The 1973 war achieved both ends: Israel came to appreciate that a treaty with Egypt was worth having, and the United States — largely as a result of the Arab oil embargo — decided that successful negotiations were vital to its interests.

The Camp David peace process began with Sadat's trip to Jerusalem in November 1977 and ended with an Egyptian-Israeli treaty in March 1979. With Israel removed as a barrier and the Sinai returned to Egypt, Sadat could nurture a close relationship with the United States — a relationship which he hoped would bring the massive amounts of economic assistance Egypt so desperately needed. Peace with Israel became an essential component of his strategy.

3.4 THE CRACKDOWN ON DISSENT. In a landmark speech to the nation on September 5, 1981, President Sadat laid bare what he said was a broad, pervasive conspiracy between Islamic fundamentalist leaders and secular political opponents to destroy Egyptian national unity and sabotage his government's domestic and foreign policies. Observing due process and existing legal mechanisms, Sadat announced a series of tough new measures to back up his dictum that the exercise of religion and politics should be kept separate.

Coming on the heels of the government's round-up of some 1,500 dissident political and religious figures, the speech contained elements that together formed a major turning point in Egypt's domestic political life. After a decade's truce, marked by latent mutual distrust and increasingly frequent bouts of rhetorical abuse, Sadat declared open war on Egypt's Islamic fundamentalist movement.

Concluding a review of the events leading up to and following the June 1981 inter-communal strife in Cairo, Sadat described a "slow and quiet fanning" of sectarian tensions which certain Muslim and Christian leaders were exploiting. He accused both major opposition political parties — the Socialist Labor Party (SLP) and the more strident National Progressive Unionist Grouping (NPUG) — of playing on these sectarian troubles and of cooperating with Islamic groups in seeking to undermine the government. In particular, he charged the Muslim Brotherhood, the SLP, and the NPUG with forming an alliance committed to sabotage his policies with regard to the peace process and Israel. Sadat stopped short of outlawing the SLP and the NPUG, but he announced that al-Shaab, the SLP organ that has served as Egypt's leading opposition newspaper, would be proscribed, along with several confessionally oriented publications.

Sadat also had harsh words for certain prominent personalities. For example, he sharply criticized Coptic Pope Shenouda III for assuming a political role in addition to his ecclesiastical functions and then withdrew government recognition of Shenouda as head of the Coptic church. But it was the leaders of Islamic groups who were the focus of Sadat's ire. In particular, he singled out Umar al-Talmassani, titular head of Egypt's Muslim Brotherhood and chief editor of the Brotherhood's now-banned al-Dawa magazine. Sadat said that Talmassani, like Shenouda, had paid no heed to Sadat's admonitions to refrain from mixing politics with religion. Instead, he said, Talmassani had plunged into political controversies, attacked the Camp David process, cast doubt on Egypt's policy of peace with Israel, voiced lies about American conspiracies against "Islamic Egypt," and acted in general as "an echo" for Libya, Syria, and the Arab rejectionists.

Some 1,536 persons were arrested during the September 1981 crackdown on secular and religious opponents, and over 3,000 more were arrested following the assassination of President Sadat in October 1981. Arrests in the wake of Sadat's assassination were targeted at Islamic fundamentalist and extremist groups, particularly those associated directly or indirectly with plots to overthrow the government. Further arrests, and some re-arrests, occurred during 1982 under the provisions of the state of emergency, but on a reduced scale.

Since November 1981, the government has announced the release of some 3,700 persons. Most of the remaining prisoners have either been indicted on specific charges or are being investigated in connection with suspected criminal violations. The great majority of detainees are associated with extremist Islamic groups. Many Egyptians view the explanation of an alleged conspiracy against the government as less than convincing voicing the fear that "overkill" could eventually backfire, impelling secular critics to seek common cause with religious extremists.

3.5 MUBARAK COMES TO POWER. In coping with the national trauma that surrounded Sadat's assassination and in moving resolutely to cow Islamic extremists and other potential security threats throughout the country, Mubarak appeared ready to emerge as a formidable leader in his own right. He vowed to preserve security and stability, to eliminate corruption, to pursue economic and political liberalization, and to tackle Egypt's haunting economic and social problems. Most Egyptians welcomed Mubarak's action agenda. The new president came across as a no-nonsense, forceful, and independent man.

But Mubarak projected few innovative ideas. Instead of developing practical, effective domestic programs, Mubarak lectured his countrymen about their need to exercise greater discipline and to work harder and more productively. The optimism and confidence which he had begun to nurture have trailed off noticeably. Clearly, he has not succeeded in capturing popular imagination or arousing public enthusiasm. Instead, something like the malaise of Sadat's final years seems to be returning. Doubts are growing not only about Mubarak's key programs but also about the man himself. Egyptians are puzzled about the personal qualities which drive Mubarak. He has given few clues about where he wants to lead Egypt or how he plans to get there. Many Egyptians wonder if he is up to the job.

What concerns many Egyptians is the prospect that allowing Egypt's burgeoning economic problems to slide unchecked might lead to a spontaneous upheaval that could not easily be controlled. There is also the fear that ominous economic or political developments might spark rebellion in the military or security services. This threat comes from the growing perception by many Egyptians that the quality of life is deteriorating sharply. To address these problems, Mubarak will need to match his government's accomplishments in preserving Egypt's domestic tranquility and political stability with effective responses to the strong desire of most Egyptians for innovation and reform.

Despite the downturn in public sentiment, it would be wrong to sell Mubarak short or to assume his days are numbered. Mubarak's long stint as Vice President and Sadat's alter ego taught him much about the exercise of power in Egypt. While he lacks the charisma of Nasser or the vision of Sadat, Mubarak knows whom he can trust in the power structure and has moved those people into positions of influence and responsibility — leaving them indebted to him. In addition, Mubarak is not a squeamish political operator. He uses his presidential power to defend his position and counter threats to his rule.

The extent to which Mubarak will take difficult decisions, ensure that they are carried out, and endure the political controversy that is sure to follow remains the critical question. He has frequently emphasized that Egypt cannot benefit from radical changes of either personalities or policies. But without a more innovative approach to Egypt's problems, Mubarak will be leading his country and himself into troubled waters.

The strong security situation Mubarak has established gives him a good base to launch a carefully conceived program of reform and reconstruction. Only in this way will he retain the support and confidence so necessary to the longevity of his government. Failure to do so will play increasingly into the hands of the government's many secular and religious opponents. Although they are much quieter now than they were in 1981, they continue to work actively behind the scenes in the hope of finding ways to profit from Mubarak's problems, miscalculations, and mistakes.

The greatest hope of most Egyptians was that Mubarak could effect changes in government policy and style and forge a leadership role that enjoyed both intellectual and popular support. In this respect, he has failed. The danger now is that his quest for stability and continuity will take precedence over the need for reform, and that he will find himself increasingly isolated, overly dependent on a few advisors, and forced to rely on repression to maintain himself in power. This would be seized upon by his political and religious opponents as an opportunity to organize challenges to the regime.

3.6 EXPERIMENTS IN DEMOCRACY. The net effect of Sadat's liberalization policies, in political terms, is an Egypt that allows an impressive degree of political freedom when judged by the standards of neighboring states, but where critics of the government are kept on a tight leash. Sadat approached liberalization with a view to maximizing freedom of expression for his supporters and minimizing it for his critics. Clearly, he never intended to permit full democracy in the Western sense of the concept. Nonetheless, Sadat believed that the majority of Egyptians supported the positions he took in domestic and foreign policies. He risked little, therefore, by giving them freedom to express their views in political parties and elections to an Assembly that does not make policy, but does serve as an influential forum for opinion. Where individuals and groups in Egypt went beyond "constructive" criticism — and Sadat often revealed himself to be thin-skinned in defining these limits — he reined them in.

Mubarak seems to hold a similar view. He appears to want greater political liberalization for Egypt, but clearly recognizes that Egypt has neither the institutions nor the degree of popular consciousness required for the effective exercise of democracy. The actions he takes are therefore rooted in the assumption that it will require generations of education before anything approaching Western-style democracy will be practiced in Egypt. Even so, he has shown a determination to begin building democratic institutions that will serve as the conduit for articulating the views and needs of the people to the government, as well as explaining the government's policies and programs to the people. At the same time, Mubarak is mindful that this building period contains the seeds of danger. The interests of the state and the people must be protected from those who might abuse their new freedoms. Thus, he is fully prepared to revert to more authoritarian methods if he senses that his primacy might come into question.

There is little doubt that large numbers of Egyptians would welcome a greater degree of political participation than they now possess, or than the government is likely to allow. There is no evidence, however, that this wish threatens the government, or that revolution is likely to be launched with democracy as its goal. In the political realm, at least, Egyptians compare their present lot with what it was previously and consider themselves ahead.

Currently, public opinion is an important ingredient in Egyptian decision-making. The government makes a considerable effort to gauge the public mood to learn which of its policies are popular, which are being criticized, and particularly which problems could cause anti-government sentiment to reach dangerous levels. In addition to regular networks of informants, the government periodically takes opinion polls that are unscientific by Western standards but which help to keep the authorities fairly well apprised of popular sentiment.

Mubarak has also given his Cabinet ministers a more regular and important role in decision-making than they had under Sadat, particularly on economic and other domestic matters. Issues are thoroughly considered in committees and sometimes in the full Cabinet. The most important Cabinet-level group is the Higher Policy Committee, which appears to have considerable authority to act on its own, although major decisions are referred to the President. The Prime Minister checks with the President before allowing the consideration of any issue to proceed very far. Decisions in the Cabinet and Higher Policy Committee – final actions as well as recommendations to the President – generally are taken by consensus rather than formal vote. The influence of the Cabinet on presidential decisions is limited by the Prime Minister who acts as an intermediary between the President and most of the Ministers. Mubarak has consistently supported the Prime Minister's efforts to head the Cabinet in fact as well as in name. Given his control of the Cabinet, the Prime Minister has the largest say, apart from the President, in making policy.

3.7 POLITICAL PARTIES. Although political parties had existed off and on in Egypt for many decades – they were banned under Nasser and all political activity subsumed within his Arab Socialist Union, then re-legalized but restricted by Sadat – the present form of the Egyptian party system reflects legislation passed only in August 1983.

Law 114 established a party list system and eliminated independent candidates. It increased the number of elected deputies from 382 to 448 with the president empowered to appoint up to ten additional delegates. Electoral districts were redrawn – there are now forty-eight districts compared to 176 in the 1979 election – making them much larger than the two- or three-member districts from which the previous Assembly deputies were elected. At least thirty-one of the districts must have a female candidate, and in all districts at least 50 percent of the seats must go to workers or peasants. The principle of proportional representation, together with the larger districts, theoretically gives opposition parties a better chance to be represented in the Assembly.

The NDP. The largest political party, established by Sadat, is the National Democratic Party (NDP). It is the "ruling" party in the sense that the President heads it and a large majority of members of parliament belong to it. It is not a cohesive political force, but instead an amorphous patronage machine that embraces a variety of viewpoints. Partly because of its internal divisions, the NDP has not placed a distinctive imprint on Egyptian policy. Opinion within the NDP can indirectly affect decisions, however, by setting general limits to policy change. If Mubarak disregarded those limits, he might face embarrassing resistance among NDP members in the People's Assembly. Most of the NDP's top leaders occupy high positions in the government.

The role of the opposition is in transition. After becoming President, Mubarak said he would meet with opposition leaders and solicit their views as part of the broader exposure that he indicated would distinguish his presidency from Sadat's. Mubarak held a series of such meetings during his first few months in office, but the sessions subsequently became less frequent. The tone of relations between Mubarak and the opposition parties has steadily worsened. Even so, the opposition parties have some indirect influence on Mubarak's decisions, since he tries to avoid moves that would give them easily exploitable issues.

The Wafd. The Wafd first emerged in 1919 as an all-embracing liberal nationalist independence movement. Although dominated by the middle class, it used a potent mix of nationalism and democratic-populism to mobilize the masses against the British. Yet the Wafd was continuously frustrated in its bid for power. Following an abortive effort by the Wafd and other political forces to forestall Nasser's authoritarian regime, all political parties were banned in 1954. In 1976 and 1977, Sadat briefly allowed the Wafd to reemerge, only to ban its leaders from political activity when they became too vigorous in attacking his rule. Finally, through court actions in October 1983 and January 1984, the Wafd was readmitted to Egyptian politics.

Although not tested at the polls since before the 1952 Revolution, the Wafd won 13 percent of the vote nationwide in the May 1984 People's Assembly election to become the only opposition party represented in that body. To broaden Wafd support, Party Chairman Fouad Siraj al-Din openly courted the Muslim Brotherhood. The Wafd has taken up Muslim Brotherhood themes on Islamization, allowed the Brotherhood to assume a leadership role in Wafd campaign activity prior to the election, and included nine prominent Brotherhood members in its party lists. For its part, the Muslim Brotherhood appears to be using the Wafd to gain entrance into the political process from which it is legally banned.

Strength of the Religious Right. Apart from the army, the religious right is potentially the strongest political force in Egypt. This latent power stems in large part from current social conditions and religious attitudes, but it has roots also in modern Egyptian history. Most Egyptians take for granted Islam's involvement in politics — though they do not necessarily approve of it — both because Islamic doctrine lacks the concept of a separation between church and state and because of the central part played by religious figures in Egypt's struggle against colonialism.

Over the past century, religious and secular nationalists have cooperated closely for short-term objectives. Their alliances have been fragile (spectacularly so in the case of the Muslim Brotherhood and the Free Officers of 1952), but they have shared a common bond in the rejection of alien western rule and values. Today this bond is greatly weakened. There is little shared philosophical ground between contemporary right-wing religious opponents of the government and its critics on the left. Indeed, the lack of communication between secular and religious opposition elements is one of the strongest cards the government holds.

Now, as in the past, the fundamental strength of the religious right lies in the piety of the Egyptian people. The mass of Egyptians, rural and urban, look to Islam for answers in material as well as spiritual matters. Deteriorating social and economic conditions contribute to the revival of Islamic fundamentalism. Egyptian religious fanatics, like their counterparts in other states, are by-products of conditions of deprivation, poverty, and inequality.

Fragmentation. The fragmentation of the fundamentalist right reduces its threat to the government. At present, the Islamic movement lacks the charismatic leadership that might transform it into a powerful opposition force and is on the defense in the face of government efforts to reduce its troublemaking capacity. The absence of a hierarchical structure in Sunni Islam argues against the rise of large-scale, organized opposition. Nevertheless, resurgent Islam has a momentum of its own; its strength is likely to grow if the root causes of current discontent — economic hardship to a large degree, but also social and political problems — continue to worsen. A government misstep in some sensitive area could provide the impetus needed to galvanize the Islamic right.

The Left. The Egyptian left, unlike the fundamentalist groups, has considerable organizational talent, but enjoys only a limited appeal among the generally conservative population. The illegal Communist movement is small, fragmented, and weak. The Socialists are larger and legal, but also too small and weak to obtain a parliamentary mandate under the current system. These and other small parties and groups on the left — legal and illegal — are riven with mutual suspicion and ideological incompatibility; they have resisted coalition and have failed to coalesce around any single powerful issue or charismatic leader. Efforts to make common cause with the Islamic right met with little success.

The left's inherent problems were compounded by President Sadat, whose attitude was hostile. He broke the growing power of the left by closing its press, harrassing its leaders, and disrupting its organizations. By focusing his main fire on the left, President Sadat opened the way for the burgeoning right, including the very extremist elements that in the end assassinated him. The left has still not recovered from Sadat's attack.

1984 Election Results. The National Democratic Party (President Mubarak's party) won 390 seats (73 percent of the vote and 87 percent of the seats) in the May 1984 People's Assembly election. The opposition Wafd Party won 58 seats (15 percent of the vote and 13 percent of the seats). None of the remaining three legal opposition parties (Socialist Labor Party; Socialist Liberal Party; National Progressive Unionist Grouping) met the requirement under Law 114 of winning at least 8 percent of the vote nationwide. The threshold had previously been at 5 percent, and there was considerable protest by the smaller parties when this was raised prior to the elections. Thus, the Wafd is the only opposition party represented in the Assembly. The Communist party and the Muslim Brotherhood are still illegal parties.

There are other features of the election worth noting: in rural areas the voter turnout was twice as high as in urban centers — and about 30 percent of registered women voted. This is a significant figure given Egypt's socially conservative nature. Moreover, the electoral laws stipulate that at least thirty-one seats must be filled by women (the party with a plurality automatically receives one of the women's seats). In fact forty women (mostly NDP) were elected to the legislature. Finally, only eighty-eight electoral violations were confirmed out of 23,000 polling stations and these violations are open to redress by the court. The implications of these statistics are significant:

- The election results fulfilled the intention of the law.
- The elections were genuinely free and relatively uncorrupt.
- The elections moved Egypt a significant step toward democracy.
- The courts reinforced this move by upholding the opposition against the government.
- President Mubarak showed himself ready to move more quickly and farther than his predecessors toward democracy: he did not take harsh measures against the opposition, he allowed free local and by-elections, and he avoided excessive promises or demagoguery, thus setting a new pattern of electioneering by a leader.
- The elections produced real grass-roots political work by the parties, including the NDP, which bodes well for the future of the electoral process in Egypt.
- President Mubarak's electoral victory firms up the forces of political stability. Should the pattern be repeated often enough, future elections could make Egyptian leaders less dependent for support on the military.

4.
RELATIONS WITH ISRAEL

4.1 BACKGROUND. Egypt's relations with Israel were shaped historically by several factors: geographical contiguity, the size and training of Egypt's army as compared to Israel, Egypt's role as leader of the Arab world, and strong domestic commitment to the Palestinian cause. Despite the relative ineffectiveness of the Egyptian army, Israel considered Egypt its most threatening enemy in each of the four Arab-Israeli wars fought from 1948 to 1973. Because the 1967 war resulted in the long-term loss of Sinai, Egyptians gained a larger and more personal stake in the resolution of the Arab-Israeli conflict.

4.2 CAMP DAVID. The Camp David Framework for Peace grew out of Egyptian frustration with the breakdown of Kissinger's shuttle diplomacy — best exemplified in the Sinai I and Sinai II agreements — and conviction of the political futility and economic folly of continued military confrontation with Israel. In November 1977, Egypt's Anwar Sadat stood before the Israeli Knesset and offered to break the psychological barriers and bring peace to the region. Israel and the western nations were ecstatic, while Palestinians and other Arabs looked on in skeptical disbelief. On December 5, 1977, most Arab states rejected Sadat's call for a Geneva peace conference. Egypt broke relations with the "Steadfastness and Confrontation Front," composed of the more hardline states of Libya, Syria, Iraq, Algeria and South Yemen.

President Sadat's offer of "peace and recognition" in exchange for "Israeli withdrawal" led promptly to a well-publicized meeting between Sadat and Prime Minister Menahem Begin at Ismailia at the end of December. Israeli rejection of the concept of total withdrawal in exchange for peace soon became apparent; all that Begin would offer was "limited self-rule" for Palestinians in "Judea and Samaria" under Israeli sovereignty and a demilitarization (without withdrawal of settlements) for Sinai. Talks dragged to a virtual halt after the March 1978 Israeli invasion of southern Lebanon. Arab countries warned that Israel would never give up the West Bank, that Sadat had been duped by Begin or was collaborating with Israel to obtain a separate peace for Egypt.

In September 1978, U.S. President Jimmy Carter invited Sadat and Begin to Camp David in the Maryland mountains for an intensive two-week negotiating session facilitated by the United States. From that meeting came a statement of principles, endorsed by the three leaders, which established that:

- within three months, Egypt and Israel would negotiate a peace treaty providing for Israeli withdrawal from Sinai and normalization of Egyptian-Israeli relations;
- the fate of the West Bank and Gaza would be determined after a five-year interim period during which an elected self-governing authority would replace the Israeli military government and negotiations would be conducted for final resolution among Israel, Jordan, Egypt, and representatives of the Palestinian people.

UN Resolutions 242 and 338 were explicitly subsumed in the Camp David Framework as the basis for a peace settlement.

Disagreement over the basic implications of the Framework surfaced before the ink was dry. Carter and Sadat stated publicly that they had an informal guarantee from Begin to suspend Israeli settlements until the entire negotiating process was complete; Begin contradicted. Further, Carter and Sadat understood that the two Frameworks were linked, while Begin negated this also.

Nonetheless, negotiations continued between Israel and Egypt. A peace treaty was signed on March 26, 1979. It provided for:

- phased Israeli withdrawal from Sinai (completed on April 9, 1982);
- end of the state of war and normalization of relations;
- confirmation of Israel's right to buy Egyptian oil;
- granting to Israel of the right to use the Suez Canal.

Five days after the treaty was signed, the PLO and eighteen Arab League nations (all except Oman, Sudan, and Somalia) broke diplomatic and economic ties with Egypt. Because the treaty contained no provision to guarantee

Palestinian self-determination, the Arab states suspended Egyptian membership in the Arab League and branded Sadat a traitor.

4.3 SADAT'S MOTIVATIONS FOR PEACE. A distinction should be made between Sadat's motives for seeking peace with Israel and those of the majority of the Egyptian populace for acquiescing to that peace. Sadat's initial intentions, which largely shaped his foreign policy, can be summarized as follows:

- ending the war drain on Egypt's economy. To establish credibility as a successor to Nasser (whose charisma he lacked), Sadat sought to become the leader who restored prosperity to Egypt;
- establishing a measure of independence from the wealthier Arab states who provided funds;
- integrating Egypt into the western-oriented bloc of nations. For this, it was necessary to disentangle Egypt from a conflict which set it at odds with the United States.

At a later stage, Sadat's strategy evidenced his desire to conform to the image of a peace-maker that the western media had created for him.

For the bulk of the Egyptian population, peace was a respite from the war that was draining Egypt's resources, making inordinate claims on the lives of its citizens, and causing it to lose control of its destiny. Despite Sadat's grandiose declarations, Egyptians were skeptical about the prospects for post-war prosperity.

Most Egyptians had little sympathy for Sadat's other objectives. Despite rivalries, Egyptians have long seen their interests as linked with their Arab neighbors. Arab condemnation of Sadat's peace initiative alienated some Egyptians, but most Egyptians found their bond to the Arab world, based on cultural affinities and the perception of a common destiny, as strong as ever.

Alliance with the west offered fewer attractions to most Egyptians than it did to Sadat. The "communist threat" was seen by Egyptians as remote and ideologically insignificant, especially given the predominance of religious feeling. Egypt's experience with foreign domination made Egyptians uncomfortable about a close relationship with a powerful partner; this lessened the attraction of a partnership with the United States. The west was also perceived (rightly or wrongly) as primarily materialistic which fostered negative feelings among Islamic groups.

Sadat's obsession with his western media image heightened the Egyptian perception that he felt inferior to his western counterparts. As he reveled in his role of international media hero, his popularity with his own people declined. His success in concluding a semblance of peace with Israel was more than eclipsed internally by the polarization of Egyptian society, setting Muslim against Christian, rich against poor. Many Egyptians, including many of Sadat's one-time supporters, reacted with a certain feeling of relief to his abrupt absence from the scene.

The peace treaty has outlived Sadat. However, Egyptians are at best lukewarm about friendly relations with Israel, which they view as a militaristic, expansionist state, whose brutal actions in Lebanon totally contradict any genuine desire for peaceful coexistence. Egyptians are largely unenthusiastic about visiting Israel or engaging in trade with Israel. The part of the treaty to which they are attached is the one suspending hostilities and the threat of conflagration — the one genuine motive Egyptians had for making peace. By being reticent about the other clauses of the treaty, Egyptians (Mubarak among them) hope to distance themselves from the consequences of the accord in the eyes of other Arabs.

It is evident that the Israelis value the treaty for precisely the fact that it has given Israel freedom of action in the Levant. They are clearly unenthusiastic in their commitment to the autonomy promised for the West Bank and Gaza in the treaty. The Egyptian-Israeli peace treaty owes its continuance to the harmony of contradictory self-interests that it embodies.

4.4 PEACE WITH ISRAEL. Even before the 1982 invasion of Lebanon, many Egyptians had serious doubts about Israel's aims. In their view, an array of actions seemed inconsistent with Israel's stated desire for a broader peace: the expansion of settlements in the West Bank and the creation of new ones; frequent forays into Lebanon; the bombing of Iraq's nuclear reactor; the dismissal of freely elected mayors in the occupied territories; the annexation of East Jerusalem and the Golan Heights; the refusal to evacuate Taba; accusations of Egyptian treaty violations immediately prior to the final withdrawal from Sinai in April 1982; the destruction left behind in the Sinai; and a general unwillingness to create an atmosphere conducive to moving the peace process forward.

Against this background, most Egyptians saw the invasion of Lebanon and the siege of Beirut as a watershed, demonstrating that Israel has no interest in peace with its other neighbors. Moreover, Israel's military exploits reinforced the belief among many Egyptians that their national interests are intertwined with those of their Arab neighbors. As a result, the Egyptian-Israeli relationship has suffered considerable damage.

Egyptians assert that the carnage Israel inflicted on Lebanon and the cumulative effect of Israeli attitudes and actions toward the Arab world are raising again the psychological barriers which began to fall after President Sadat's visit to Jerusalem. At the same time, Egyptian officials insist that Egypt is adhering, and will continue to adhere, to the letter of her treaty commitments. Nevertheless, they ask how Egypt can be expected to deal with Israel as though nothing had happened to increase Arab-Israeli tensions elsewhere in the region and particularly as though nothing had happened in Lebanon. In Egyptian eyes, Israel is in violation of the spirit of Camp David, and therefore bears primary responsibility for the setback to Egyptian-Israeli relations.

As for the Palestinian issue, the Egyptian leadership continues to appeal to the Palestinians to join the peace process before it is too late. But, while speaking warmly of Egypt's devotion to and desire to serve the Palestinian cause, Mubarak has put Arafat and other PLO officials squarely on notice that there can be no retreat from the Camp David Accords or the Egyptian-Israeli Peace Treaty.

4.5 THE FUTURE OF NORMALIZATION. Egyptian officials maintain that the state of Egypt's bilateral relations with Israel depends on a range of issues, as is the case with relations between all nations. To the Egyptians, the peace treaty spelled out the minimum requirements for peaceful coexistence, and Egypt has tried faithfully to meet these requirements. But instead of looking only to the treaty, Egypt places great importance on developments in the peace process, and Israel's actions toward other Arab states and the Palestinians, as fundamental components governing the evolution of the Egyptian-Israeli bilateral relationship. To the Egyptians, the peace treaty is something to build on by dint of trust and goodwill; it is not a guarantee of a brotherly embrace or of a special relationship.

During the period between April 25, 1982 (the return of the Sinai) and June 6, 1982 (the invasion of Lebanon), Egypt and Israel had begun to explore economic, commercial, and other aspects of their bilateral relationship. This process came to a halt during the summer when Israeli intentions toward Lebanon became evident. Since June 6, Egypt has selectively used the diplomatic, economic and commercial relationship to express her displeasure over Israel's behavior. Egypt recalled its ambassador from Tel Aviv and has not yet returned him.

Egypt has allowed most of the previously existing arrangements to remain in place, but has not allowed ties to grow. Moreover, Egypt has resisted vigorously Israeli overtures for new bilateral activities, arguing that the atmosphere between the two countries must first be improved by Israeli withdrawal from Lebanon and by a new Israeli attitude toward the West Bank.

Although Egypt and Israel undertook to establish normal economic, commercial, and cultural relations under processes set forth in the peace treaty and Annex III, most normalization obligations are governed by the 40-odd agreements and other documents signed by the two governments since 1979. These relate to civil aviation, transportation, tourism, trade, communications, agriculture, and culture. All include elements of discretion and are often vague enough to be subject to varying interpretations. The result is a gray area that gives both sides ample room to trade charges and countercharges about violations of Camp David and the peace treaty.

Trade, except for oil sales, has dwindled to almost nothing, expressing Egypt's displeasure with Israel. The Israelis cite the lack of trade as a treaty violation, while the Egyptians say the lack of trade is an understandable reaction to events in Lebanon.

5. RELATIONS WITH THE ARAB WORLD

5.1 PERCEPTIONS OF EGYPTIAN LEADERSHIP. Egyptians possess a sense of national identity unsurpassed by Arabs of other nationalities. They see themselves as the heirs of a cultural tradition stretching back thousands of years. Although Egyptians feel a common bond with the many Islamic nations throughout the world, and a particular tie with their Arab "brothers," they consider themselves superior.

Egypt is the most populous of any of the Arab nations and has supplied skilled workers to neighboring Arab states. Despite the deterioration of its military equipment, Egypt has the strongest army and has dramatically proved its willingness to take to the battlefield against the Israelis. As the seat of al-Azhar University, Egypt considers itself the intellectual center of Islam. It has played a leading role in the non-aligned movement and has an influential voice in African affairs. Egyptians tend to assume that these credentials ought to, by right, establish their claim as the preeminent Arab state.

5.2 RELATIONS WITH THE SAUDIS. Of Egypt's neighbors, Saudi Arabia is the most important. Tracing the course of Egyptian-Saudi relations over the past decade provides a perspective on Egypt's experience in leadership and isolation among the Arabs.

Seeds for the enhancement of Egyptian-Saudi relations were sown after the retreat of Nasser's expeditionary forces from Yemen in 1967. Egyptian-Saudi friendship flowered after the October 1973 war and reached full bloom just prior to Sadat's unilateral gesture to the Israelis, capped by his trip to Jerusalem in 1977. For almost half a decade, Cairo and Riyadh were partners in the political and economic development of the region.

The Egyptian-Saudi relationship had to weather a few storms for five years following the 1973 war. The Saudis did not criticize the Sinai disengagement agreements between Egypt and Israel, and after the Sadat initiative of

November 1977, the Saudis elected not to join the Arab rejectionist front states at the summits in Tripoli, Libya (December 1977) and in Algiers (February 1978). Even after the signing of the Camp David agreements in September 1978, the hard-line elements in the House of Saud did not prevail, but then came the pan-Arab conferences and the turning point.

5.3 EGYPT'S ISOLATION. Resolutions emanating from the Baghdad summits of November 1978 and March 1979 ostracized Egypt and imposed economic and political sanctions against it to punish Sadat for his independence. In effect, the signing of the Egyptian-Israeli treaty of peace compelled the Saudis to toe the prevailing pan-Arab line in order to forestall what could have been a polarization of the Arab world into western and anti-western camps.

The Iranian revolution, which sent shock waves throughout the Islamic world, forced the Saudis and other moderate Arabs to reassess their domestic and foreign policies. The foremost lesson of Iran, for the Arabs who sought to understand it, appeared to be that overt and substantial reliance on the United States (or for that matter on the Soviet Union) would not be acceptable Islamic policy. The maintenance of political and economic sovereignty, undefiled by foreign influence, became the criterion by which the Islamic peoples would judge the acceptability of their rulers. The Iranian revolution served to reinforce the dictum that without the support of the masses, the ruling regime will eventually topple.

As one of the few remaining Islamic dynastic monarchies, the Saudi political elite took warning and began to set its house in order. The break with Egypt in April 1979 was one of the first, clear indications that the Saudis were reassessing their political alignments in the region. It was a relatively painless way for the Saudis to symbolically distance themselves from an evolving prowestern alliance system in the region. However, the decisions to sever relations, to cancel the purchase of $525 million in F5E aircraft for Egypt, and to terminate the Egyptian-based military-industrial undertaking known as the Arab Organization for Industrialization were made with the foreknowledge that Sadat would not be left out in the cold. He had, after all, an alternative and potentially greater source of aid: the United States.

5.4 A LOW POINT IN RELATIONS. The peace treaty with Israel — along with Sadat's tendency not only to ignore

Arab sensibilities but to aggravate existing strains with gratuitous insults — brought Egypt's relations with the Arab world to the lowest point in modern history and cost Egypt its leadership role.

- Egypt was suspended or expelled from all pan-Arab and Islamic organizations.
- Diplomatic relations were severed with every Arab country except Oman, Sudan, and Somalia, although almost all left their embassy staffs in place.
- The Arab League and its subsidiary organizations pulled out of Cairo.
- Various economic sanctions were voted, but many have been sidestepped or applied in such fashion as not to burden the sanctioning states excessively.
- Egypt has received no new government-to-government aid from the Arabs since the treaty was concluded in March 1979.

Egypt's willingness to engage Israel in the Palestinian autonomy negotiations and to pursue normalization of relations has been reciprocated by a series of Israeli actions which have embarrassed the Egyptians further in the eyes of Arabs, Muslims and domestic public opinion. The net result has been Egypt's isolation from the Arab mainstream, doubt about the soundness of Mubarak's policies, and an erosion of the Government's domestic support.

Arab moderates feel that Sadat backed himself into a corner by being too close to the United States and Israel, by being brutally insulting to the Arabs who rejected the Camp David process, and by attaching his prestige to a cause "doomed by Israeli intransigence." Moreover, Sadat set the price for reconciliation with Egypt so high that no Arab moderate could afford it.

Mubarak, however, is not tarred by Sadat's actions and can, without penalty, carry out plans which he inherited — perhaps with cosmetic changes to make them more palatable. Given the personal nature of Sadat's alienation, Arabs who would never have forgiven Sadat could accept Mubarak if he handles himself well — even if he remains involved in the peace process. In these circumstances, Mubarak might not have to repudiate anything Sadat did or said, so long as he remains attentive to the sensitivities of key Arab leaders and, on occasion, "gets tough" with the Israelis.

Nevertheless, leading government officials repeatedly have asserted that Egypt is committed to the accords it signed with Israel and that Egypt is not willing to pay a prohibitive price to get back into the good graces of the

Arabs at any cost. This continues to be a precept of Egyptian policy. It has not prevented the development of good working relations with some Arab countries, but it remains an obstacle to the resumption of full political and diplomatic ties.

The Egyptians were bitterly disappointed with Saudi Arabia's performance at the Fez Summit in September 1982 when the question of relations with Egypt arose. The Egyptians believe that King Fahd is more interested in promoting an Arab consensus to tackle the various peace initiatives than in risking further divisions among the Arabs by supporting Egypt's reintegration. Moreover, many Egyptians suspect the Saudis do not want to risk their growing political power among the Arabs by again having to compete with Egypt's traditional leadership role. Most Egyptians remain uncertain whether Saudi Arabia is yet ready to see Egypt rejoin the Arab fold, and conclude that countries dependent on the Saudis either financially or politically will follow the Saudi lead.

Even so, Egypt's contacts with the other Arabs have increased considerably since Mubarak took power. While a public rapprochement is inevitable, the process is likely to be gradual and vulnerable to events in the region.

5.5 STEPS TOWARD REINTEGRATION.

Egypt has been remarkably successful during the past year in trying to reintegrate itself into the Arab and Islamic worlds. However, outright Syrian and Libyan opposition and Saudi ambivalence will continue to pose obstacles as long as the Arab League operates on the basis of consensus.

Egypt's election to the United Nations Security council in November 1983, Mubarak's meeting with Arafat in December 1983, and the Islamic conference decision to readmit Egypt in March 1984 greatly strengthened Mubarak's domestic position and increased Egyptian confidence in the direction of his foreign policy. Growing Arab concern over the course of the Iran-Iraq war and about Syrian ascendancy in the region have added to the momentum for Egyptian reintegration.

Arab states are reluctant, however, to restore full relations until Egypt is readmitted to the Arab League, and progress in the League is blocked by the need for consensus. Syria and Libya strongly oppose restoration of Arab ties to Egypt while the peace treaty with Israel remains in effect — and Egypt has no intention of going back on the treaty. In addition to fearing Syrian and Libyan subversion, many Arab states are influenced by Damascus' argument that the peace treaty greatly enhanced

Israel's strategic position. Saudi Arabia, which sees itself as the custodian of the Arab consensus, continues to believe that Egypt was mistaken in trying to represent the Palestinians. The Saudis have indefinitely postponed the Arab summit previously scheduled to take place in Riyadh in March 1984 in order to avoid an open confrontation over the Egyptian issue.

Given the continuing lack of Arab consensus, few Arab states are likely to restore full relations with Egypt unilaterally unless one of them makes a bold move. King Hussein's restoration of relations in late September 1984 may have opened the way for others. The stout support of Egypt and Jordan in its war with Iran could provide the common ground on which Saddam Hussein would feel secure enough to restore Iraqi-Egyptian relations. Such an act could combine with Saudi security apprehensions about the Gulf to warrant a similar move by Riyadh or action by the Saudis which would trigger a wider Arab effort toward reintegrating Egypt into the Arab camp.

Egyptian diplomacy in the short term is likely to focus on promoting Jordanian-Palestinian participation in the peace process, discreet contacts with Syria, Libya, and Saudi Arabia, and a Jordanian proposal to amend the Arab Leaguge charter to allow for a majority decision by secret ballot. For the time being, Egypt seems satisfied with the nature of its Arab ties and is anxious not to appear the supplicant.

5.6 EGYPT'S DIPLOMATIC ROLE IN THE IRAN-IRAQ WAR.

Egypt's diplomatic activity to garner support for its initiative among Non-Aligned Movement (NAM) states to end the Gulf war not only aims at breaking the present logjam but also at regaining the international standing Egypt enjoyed prior to the peace treaty with Israel. However, the initiative probably is a non-starter, and Egyptian prestige will suffer if Egypt's hard-sell tactics lead to disunity in the NAM.

The initiative relies heavily on points previously announced by the Islamic peace committee. Egypt proposes: (1) an immediate ceasefire, (2) withdrawal to international boundaries, (3) the interposition of an international peacekeeping force, (4) the convening of an international tribunal to determine the aggressor in the war, (5) the creation of a war indemnity fund with as much as $40 million donated by Arab states and earmarked primarily for Iran, and (6) the enforcement of the 1975 treaty, a point calculated to convince Iran that Iraq will gain nothing from the war.

The chances that the initiative will succeed are virtually nonexistent. Egypt has consistently supported Iraq with military sales and the provision of expertise, while it has no relations with Iran. In turn, Iran insists on its original demands as the price for peace, including the ouster of Saddam Hussein and the Baath party. Recently, signs have emerged that Iran is disenchanted with the NAM as a whole, and is accusing it of having an Iraqi bias. This will further frustrate Egyptian efforts to work through the NAM.

In addition to enhancing its image as an international peace-maker, Egypt hopes to gain other benefits. The attempt by Egypt to extricate Iraq from the war might move some of the Arab states closer to restoring formal diplomatic ties with Egypt. Moreover, Egypt might regain the dominant position it once had as one of the three co-founders of the NAM, if the initiative succeeded. Domestically, Mubarak would be able to cite his ability as an international statesman, notwithstanding Egypt's ostracism by the Arabs.

Reaction from NAM members has been muted. Most NAM states will accept the Egyptian initiative as long as they do not have to participate in any substantive fashion. India especially, as Chairman of the NAM, wants to avoid splits within that body; it does not want an initiative that has no chance of success and that might force India to take sides. Part of the reason for Mrs. Gandhi's cancellation of her proposed April visit to Cairo may have been the desire to avoid a formal discussion of the plan with Mubarak. Thus, it is unlikely that Egypt's initiative will form the basis for any bid by the NAM at mediation in the war. Egypt, nonetheless, can claim that it tried.

5.7 RELATONS WITH LIBYA AND THE SUDAN. Egypt's relations with neighboring Libya and the Sudan offer perhaps the starkest contrast between intra-Arab emnity and amity anywhere in the Arab world. Relations with Libya soured ever since Libyan President Muammar Qaddafi led Arab opposition to Sadat's policies of peace with Israel and cooperation with the United States, calling for Sadat's ouster as an Arab traitor. Things have not improved in the Mubarak era. Both Egypt and Libya appear at present to be funneling aid to opposition groups seeking the overthrow of each other's government. The Sudan, Oman and Somalia on the other hand, were the only Arab countries not to break diplomatic relations with Egypt over the treaty with Israel. During Mubarak's rule, the Sudan's

President Numeiry has aligned himself even more closely with his downstream Nile neighbor and has led efforts to reintegrate Egypt in Arab and Islamic forums.

Libyan efforts to oust the Numeiry regime in the Sudan have perhaps caused Egypt more concern than Tripoli's denunciation of Egyptian policy toward Israel. In addition to increasing Cairo's alienation from Tripoli, the Libyan threat to the Sudan has also been a major factor prompting closer Egyptian-Sudanese ties. A 1976 coup attempt by Libyan-backed Sudanese insurgents that resulted in several days of fighting and left hundreds of Sudanese dead was quickly followed by an Egyptian-Sudanese defense pact. The agreement provided for the permanent stationing of an unspecified number of Egyptian troops near the Sudanese capital, Khartoum. Although Egypt reacted skeptically to American and Sudanese reports of threatening Libyan troop movements in February 1983, Cairo was quick to join the Sudan in accusing Libya of sending a lone plane to bomb Omduran in April 1984, and approved the dispatch of two American AWACs and support aircraft to the Sudan. The Egyptians have thus appeared not to exaggerate or dramatize Libyan threats to their interests, but they have at the same time been quick to mount effective opposition to Libyan movements.

Libya's military intervention in Chad also brought swift Egyptian and Sudanese denunciations, first in December 1980, and again following the deepening of Libyan involvement in 1983. Cairo condemned the Qaddafi regime for allegedly backing anti-government groups such as the subversive cells uncovered by Egyptian security authorities in April 1983.

Subversive pressures from Libya (and to a lesser extent from Ethiopia) were one of the main reasons behind President Numeiry's initiative in seeking to reinforce his earlier defense pact with Cairo with an agreement to "integrate" Egypt and the Sudan. He and President Mubarak signed a "charter for integration" on October 12, 1982, calling for the unification of defense, economic, and social policies over the following decade. The integration agreement provided for the abolition of visas and work permits between the two countries and the dropping of duties on agricultural produce. The bureaucratic apparatus for the integration — a Secretary General, an Integration Fund, and Standing Technical Committees — was set up in February 1983 and the first session of the "Nile Valley Parliament" was held three months later. Both local and foreign analysts, however, doubt that the large-scale joint development schemes envisioned will be implemented or that the integration will progress to a de facto union.

Sudanese memory of Egyptian colonial rule and the special opposition of non-Muslim Sudanese to any union with Egypt is likely to be more than enough to offset the apparent complementarity of manpower (Egypt) and natural resources (the Sudan) of the two countries. Sudanese dissidents, including those not actually opposed to the Numeiry regime, already speak with rancor of the "Finlandization" of Sudanese politics within Egypt's embrace.

Still, because of both natural history and current regional politics, Egyptian-Sudanese cooperation will remain close. Moreover, Egyptian relations with both Libya and the Sudan will continue to be largely a product of the reciprocal interactions of all three members of the large and important northeast Africa triangle.

6. RELATIONS WITH THE SUPERPOWERS

6.1 RELATIONS WITH THE UNITED STATES. United States-Egyptian relations are closer and more intertwined politically, psychologically, economically, militarily, and strategically than at any time in the history of the two nations. The re-orientation of Egypt away from the Soviet Union has meant a re-orientation toward the United States. Since the Soviet expulsion and the cut off of Arab funds, the United States has become Egypt's most important financial backer. The size of the U.S. aid program to Egypt is staggering: $0.91 billion in fiscal year 1977, $0.94 billion in 1978, $2.39 billion in 1979, $1.17 billion in 1980, $1.12 billion in 1981, $1.7 billion in 1982, $2.1 billion in 1983, and $2.3 billion in 1984. Except for Israel, it is in dollar terms the largest bilateral economic assistance program in the history of U.S. aid. Egypt and the United States have developed a major mutual stake in sustaining the new direction in Egyptian policy initiated during the decade Sadat was in power:

- ending Egyptian dependence on the Soviets;
- leading the Arab world toward peace with Israel, beginning with peace between Egypt and Israel;
- liberalizing the Egyptian economy as a means of accelerating economic development (with vast amounts of U.S. aid); and
- liberalizing the political system with the goal of creating durable democratic institutions.

Mubarak is concerned that U.S. election-year politics will impede progress in the peace process. He believes that Egypt's ability to influence Israel on the Palestinian issue is nil, and that U.S. backing for Jordanian-Palestinian participation in the peace process is essential to regional stability and further improvement in Egypt's relations with the Arab states. There is a growing sense among some influential Egyptian circles — e.g. professionals, journalists, academics, and politicians — that in the final analysis, the United States simply cannot be relied upon to change its policies toward Israel, that the Israeli influence in American politics is too great for any administration to overcome, and therefore Egypt is in danger of falling into a serious political trap. These Egyptian critics are growing increasingly restless over Egypt's continued separation from the Arab camp and believe that Egypt should soon take initiatives to lead the "moderate" Arab states toward formulating an Arab solution to the Israeli-Palestinian problem. They believe such a move would not result in alienation from the United States or a reduction in U.S. aid.

6.2 RELATIONS WITH THE SOVIET UNION. Egyptian-Soviet relations, which under Nasser brought the Soviets naval and air bases in Egypt and considerable support for Soviet political aims, declined dramatically during the Sadat era. Sadat's massive purge of pro-Soviet figures from the Egyptian political establishment in May 1971 shook the Soviet leadership. Following several trips to the Soviet Union in 1971 and 1972 in a futile search for more sophisticated weapons, Sadat announced his decision to terminate the Soviet military presence in Egypt and expelled 15,000 Russians during the summer of 1972. When Egypt launched the 1973 war, the Soviets offered Sadat several gestures of support, but were slow to resupply Egypt with arms and spare parts.

Extremely irritated at sitting in the wings while Secretary Kissinger performed on center stage, the Soviets quickly joined the chorus of Arab disapproval of the first and second Sinai disengagement agreements. By March 1976, Sadat felt confident enough to abrogate the treaty of friendship and cooperation with Moscow and to deny the Soviets use of port facilities in Alexandria. In August 1977, Sadat cut off shipments of cotton and then, in September, unilaterally imposed a 10-year moratorium on Egypt's military debts to the USSR.

In 1978, Sadat ordered closed all Soviet and east bloc consulates and cultural centers outside Cairo. In response to the Soviet invasion of Afghanistan, he ordered a drastic reduction of Soviet embassy personnel in Cairo in January 1980, explaining his decision in terms of wanting to decrease Soviet assets and thereby the Soviet capacity for subversion.

The Egyptian Cabinet announced on September 15, 1981 that the Soviet Ambassador to Egypt, six Soviet embassy employees, and a Hungarian embassy employee were declared persona non grata and would be expelled. The Cabinet also ordered the closure of the Egyptian military attache's office in Moscow, the cancellation of the contracts of all Soviet experts in Egypt, the deportation of two Soviet journalists, and a general reduction of Soviet embassy personnel. These decisions were taken the same day the government announced that Soviet and east bloc intelligence services and local communist groups were engaged in activities to exploit sectarian tensions and "foment sedition" against the state.

Since then relations have improved. The announcement in April 1984 that Egypt and the Soviet Union agreed in principle to exchange ambassadors reflects Mubarak's long-standing position that Egypt must maintain ties with both superpowers. However, the Egyptians did not commit themselves on timing, and Mubarak will be careful to select a moment that will not be read as an endorsement of Soviet aims in the Middle East.

The visit to Egypt by the director of the Middle East Department of the Soviet Ministry of Foreign Affairs was the occasion for the announcement. His trip reflects Moscow's interest in ending an anomalous situation. Mubarak, as well, considers ambassadorial relations with the Soviets to be "normal," particularly now, when Egypt is attempting to strengthen its credentials in the Non-Aligned Movement. Egypt, Mubarak has implied, should be able to follow India's lead and have a special relationship with one superpower while maintaining correct ambassadorial relations with the other. Even so, any criticism of Egypt by the Soviets (as in October 1983) or an offending action by the Kremlin (a massive offensive in Afghanistan, for example) could easily cancel the progress made to date.

Egypt is in no hurry to upgrade relations. It obtained a trade agreement with Moscow (May 1983), signed a cultural-scientific protocol (April 1983), and is increasing its purchase of spare parts needed to keep its aging Soviet military equipment operational. The concrete benefits from these exchanges have accrued principally to Egypt.

One condition for an exchange of ambassadors that Mubarak will have to soft-pedal is his demand that Moscow cease its interference in Egypt's internal affairs. This demand entails an embarrassing Soviet acknowledgment that they have indeed interfered. Mubarak remains committed to thwarting Soviet advances in the region. Though upgraded relations with the USSR may give him greater flexibility to reduce his reliance on the United States if this becomes a domestic or regional liability, it is highly unlikely that Egypt's special relationship with the United States will be disrupted.

6.3 THE DANGER OF ALLIANCE. Egypt for Egyptians – not for other Arabs and certainly not for foreigners – was a consistent theme of Sadat's presidency. It underlay Sadat's decision to expel more than 15,000 Soviet military personnel in July 1972, and it underlies Mubarak's resistance to U.S. "bases" on Egyptian soil.

The growth of Soviet forces stationed in Egypt, especially those operating for exclusively Soviet purposes, became a grave affront to Egyptian national pride. What began in 1955, when the Soviets first extended significant quantities of military and economic aid, developed to the point of an Egypt dotted with small islands under Soviet extraterritorial privilege. The USSR was Egypt's primary source of war materiel in both the 1956 and 1967 wars. Apparently in return for replacing the military equipment lost in the 1967 war and for continuing other forms of assistance, the Soviets were granted use of several Egyptian air and naval facilities. The Soviets stationed anti-submarine warfare and naval reconnaissance aircraft at these Egyptian airfields and used the naval bases to support extended deployment for their ships in the Mediterranean.

During the 1969-1970 "War of Attrition," the Soviets increased their presence in Egypt five-fold, at Nasser's request, providing interceptor pilots, air defense missile troops, air defense support units, and large quantities of advanced air defense equipment for their own and Egyptian use. Soviet personnel manned missile and radar sites, flew fighter-interceptor missions against Israeli aircraft, and participated directly in command and control of the national air defense system.

Nevertheless, there was substantial friction between Egyptian and Soviet military men in both personal and professional dimensions. The highest levels of the Egyptian military were growing progressively more worried that Egypt was slipping into the status of a satellite. The Soviets erred tactically as well, for they ignored Egypt's pride, showed contempt for its character, and endeavored with insufficient finesse to subvert key sectors of its society – accruing all the while the hostility of the populace.

By some accounts, Sadat's decision to expel the Soviets came primarily because of a final Soviet refusal to provide "offensive" arms or to permit Egypt to attack Israeli forces in the Sinai. But equally important, Sadat was under heavy pressure from his military and prominent political figures to end Egypt's dependence on the Soviets. In these circumstances, Sadat took a step that would show his countrymen he was a solicitous defender of Egyptian dignity and independence.

Today, a troubling theme emerging in Islamic, independent opposition, and left-wing circles is that Egypt seems to be substituting American imperialism for Russian imperialism — militarily, economically, and culturally. The greatest criticism has been directed at the U.S.-Egyptian military relationship, with concern that Egypt is viewed by Washington as a key element in the "strategic consensus," i.e., as an agent for U.S. regional defense policies.

Sadat was out in front of his people in urging an aggressive response to the "Soviet threat" and in offering the use of Egyptian facilities to U.S. forces involved in such a response. However, Sadat was careful to assure his people that he did not plan to offer permanent "bases" to the United States, or to compromise Egypt's sovereignty as had happened in the course of Egypt's heavy reliance on the Soviet Union. Mubarak has moved no less cautiously on this issue.

On the other hand, the U.S.-Egyptian relationship might deepen to promote U.S. strategic interests, depending in large part on U.S. policies toward Egypt and its approach to the Arab-Israeli conflict. The United States has a large reservoir of good will to draw on, but the mood in Egypt raises some warning flags that suggest the United States should be sensitive to Mubarak's problems and careful not to push too hard on too many fronts. A military "alliance" with the United States is not what most Egyptians want, nor will Egypt act as a military or political surrogate for the United Staes in the region.

7.
RELATIONS WITH EUROPE AND THE THIRD WORLD

7.1 THE WEST. Reliance on the United States was not without its perils for Sadat, a self-styled critic of Nasser's over-dependence on the Soviet Union. The Iranian Revolution vividly demonstrated that even a construed commonality of interests between patron and client contained no assurances of domestic acquiescence and stability. Equating local political and security interests with those of a superpower would involve risks. But Sadat had few misgivings in accepting larger doses of U.S. aid. Egypt tempers this dependence by diversifying its aid sources to include the World Bank, Canada, Japan, and Egypt's traditional west European supporters — West Germany, France, and the United Kingdom.

7.2 CHINA. Egyptians see a strong community of interests with the Chinese on bilateral and regional issues. Both countries oppose Soviet or Soviet-supported encroachments in Southeast Asia and the Middle East. Egypt strongly supports China's positions on Vietnam and Kampuchea. The Egyptians and Chinese alike urge the United States to react more vigorously to Soviet threats to the Middle East, particularly in the Persian Gulf. Both countries support moderates in the non-aligned movement.

The military supply relationship between Egypt and China consists mainly of hard currency purchases of Chinese hardware by Egypt. Most of this hardware is technologically antiquated but for Egypt affordable and, due to its similarity to Egypt's large inventory of Soviet equipment, easy to assimilate and maintain.

Egypt seems satisfied with China's strong support for the peace process, understanding Chinese reluctance to endorse without reservation the Camp David framework because of its failure to deal with the Palestinian and Jerusalem problems in a way which satisfies other Arab interests. China's Palestinian policy, nevertheless, meshes well with Egypt's, despite the differences in timing and tactics. Both Egyptians and Chinese stress that strong bilateral political ties stem from "identical" regional and international interests.

7.3 THIRD WORLD RELATIONS. Egypt plays a leadership role in Third World politics as a prominent member of the non-aligned movement. It verbally supports SWAPO in Namibia and has denounced South Africa. In other conflicts Egypt has supported the efforts of international or regional organizations toward conflict resolution. In particular it has supported OAU attempts to resolve the dispute over the Western Sahara.

In Africa, Egyptian expertise is in demand. Egyptian technical advisers are presently working in the Cameroon, Sierre Leone and Senegal. Senegal has signed a special technical agreement for the exchange of radio and tevision programs. Kenya has sent a military delegation to Egypt and it is likely that Egyptians will participate in the development of Kenya's military forces.

Egypt is expanding trade ties with the Third World. It has renewed a tripartite agreement covering trade and cooperation in shipping, industry, technology, and development of the service sector with India and Yugoslavia. A trade protocol was also signed with North Korea aimed at increasing bilateral trade.

Egypt recently severed diplomatic ties with Costa Rica and El Salvador as a consequence of their relocation of their embassies in Israel to Jerusalem.

8.
FUTURE PROSPECTS

8.1 MUBARAK'S HOLD ON POWER. During his six years as Egypt's Vice President, Mubarak proved to be a tough political infighter with an instinct for survival. As President, he has shown himself to be no less a master than his predecessor at manipulating the complex personal rivalries and power relationships of Egypt's traditional political establishment. Although Mubarak is vulnerable on many counts, his skill at maneuvering and the resources available to him should serve him well in maintaining his hold on power.

8.2 IMPLICATIONS OF THE PEOPLE'S ASSEMBLY ELECTION. The May 1984 People's Assembly election was the first popular test of Mubarak's leadership. In the past year, Mubarak's pragmatic approach to governing, modest lifestyle, foreign policy successes, and attention to domestic issues have won him general support among the public and lessened his image as an indecisive man. Mubarak clearly hoped that the election would give him an added measure of popular legitimacy. But voter turnout was light (about 42 percent of those registered) and many of the ballots cast for the opposition parties were not so much votes for the opposition's philosophy and programs as they were votes against the government. The election results are not likely to have a profound influence on Mubarak's approach to national policy, but he may feel the need to move more cautiously than he would have wanted.

Having allowed opposition elements greater freedom, Mubarak will be less able than before to control the national debate — significant in a country where the parameters of political activity have always been narrow. He will have to deal with a reinforced opposition, led by the Wafd with significant Muslim Brotherhood support. Though the opposition will not have the power to block government policies, much less implement its own agenda, it will be able to dissent vocally from policies it does not like. Mubarak is likely to feel more constrained in this freer political climate where ignoring his critics could have potentially damaging results. This could affect the government's handling of such sensitive issues as economic reform, relations with Israel, and strategic cooperation with the United States. To the extent the government is called to account by a larger, critical Assembly opposition, Mubarak will feel less confident about getting too far out in front of popular opinion. He may well borrow a page from the American book to cite his problems with the People's Assembly to justify his inability to take certain actions of interest to the United States.

8.3 LOOMING PROBLEMS. Stormier times lie ahead if the government fails to heed the signs of warning.

- Economic progress as seen by the average Egyptian has not kept pace with expectations. Moreover, the 3 percent per annum population growth and the related problems of rising unemployment and rapid urbanization will lead to a decline in standard of living over the next 20 years or so. No combination of wise leadership, foreign assistance, and luck is likely to alter this prospect.

- The byproducts of rapid population growth will reinforce and accelerate sociopolitical changes already taking place: the rapid increase in the share of the population with middle class credentials and aspirations; the division of the middle class between civilian and military public sector employees; the greatly increased number of secondary school and college graduates who fail to achieve positions of prestige or influence; the rising educational level of the average Egyptian, making him better informed of conditions both in Egypt and elsewhere, more demanding that the government serve his interests, and perhaps less likely to follow Egypt's pharaonic tradition of giving allegiance to whoever is in power.

- How far militant Islamic fundamentalism has spread in Egypt is not clear. There is a fundamentalist opposition to virtually all government policies. The September 1981 crackdown did not eradicate this opposition. On the contrary, the religious opposition may be tempted to make common cause with the secular left. Mubarak will have to toe a careful line between tough measures to keep the lid on subversive elements that feed on frustration and anti-western currents in Egyptian society, and giving the Egyptian people confidence that there will be no return to the repression of the Nasser era.

- During the next five years, the increase in the share of economic output that must be diverted from consumption to investment to cope with rapid population growth will tend to increase social tension and strain. This will be especially so as the urban populace comes to realize not only that few post-peace increases in consumption are possible, but also that further sacrifices will be necessary.

- While the formal aspects of peace with Israel have gone forward on schedule, there is little enthusiasm for further normalization of relations. The Israeli invasion of Lebanon severely strained all aspects of the relationship. Mubarak will have to find ways to contain the deterioration of Egypt's relations with Israel both for the sake of peace itself and because of the interconnection with U.S.-Egyptian relations. This will be a difficult task.

8.4 EGYPTIAN SOVEREIGNTY AND THE UNITED STATES. The largest potential cause for trouble in U.S.-Egyptian relations lies in the character of the strategic relationship Egypt is developing with the United States. The Egyptian government has made clear its eagerness to cooperate with the United States, and in large measure is supported by Egyptian public opinion. But Egyptian leaders have also made clear that there are definite limits to the kinds of assistance and cooperation they are able to supply. "Facilities" to be used in times of crisis are acceptable but "bases," as in the use of the Sinai for regional military purposes, are not. Attempts to push the Egyptians beyond these limits would result in a crisis in bilateral relations.

8.5 ISLAMIC FUNDAMENTALISM. The Egyptian government does not face an immediate threat from the turn toward fundamentalism in general or from extremist Islamic groups in particular. The extremists have no broad popular following and no common vision of what should lie beyond the present social order, were it to be overthrown. Moreover, the general public views the extremists as a threat and supports the government's move to control them. Over the longer term, however, Mubarak will face a challenge from the appeal of Islam. He will have to find ways to persuade the Egyptian people that his government is genuinely determined to come to grips with the underlying frustrations on which radicalism and violence feed — frustrations which have their roots largely in the economic conditions under which most Egyptians live. Further, the closer Mubarak draws to the United States and Israel, the more sensitive he will have to be to providing Islamic justifications for his policies.

8.6 BUREAUCRACY AND CORRUPTION. In addition to a lack of real resources, the government's ability to address problems is limited by institutional weaknesses, especially a flaccid, inefficient, bloated bureaucracy and considerable corruption. The bureaucracy has grown so large that in many cases it barely functions. Anyone dealing with it is quickly frustrated. Corruption is widely assumed to extend to the highest levels of the Egyptian government and society. Unlike many members of Sadat's entourage, however, Mubarak is generally regarded as honest. As a result he is in a strong position to move against corruption and has already made some governmental changes on that score, but will continue to take a cautious approach.

8.7 THE DANGER OF RISING EXPECTATIONS. On balance, the lot of the average Egyptian in a strictly economic sense is improving. Yet this fact, paradoxically, is increasing rather than reducing public discontent. Exaggerated expectations of the immediate benefits of peace are an often cited factor. More precisely, the Egyptian people are aware that things can get better, but are impatient with the pace and uncertainties of progress. Increasing stratification of income, opportunity, and privilege — almost inevitable concomitants of economic liberation — add fuel to the popular mood. The gap between rich and poor is seen to be growing rapidly.

8.8 MAINTAINING THE ECONOMIC AND POLITICAL MOMENTUM. Continued stability in this setting depends greatly on the economic and political momentum Mubarak is able to generate in the conduct of Egypt's affairs, and thus is subject to constant reassessment by the public. Unquestionably, Mubarak faces a difficult road, but as long as he keeps the allegiance of the military, his chances of weathering the problems are good. Most Egyptians will be prepared to give him the chance to prove he can lead them to prosperity. As long as he can show movement in this direction, the public is likely to support him, but not uncritically.

8.9 THE ECONOMY. Although the current economic situation is far from comfortable, it is not yet desperate. Through a combination of squeezing imports and increased foreign borrowing, the government managed to cover its 1982 balance of payments deficit of slightly more that $3 billion and its 1983 deficit of about $1.3 billion. But Egypt is finding it increasingly difficult to borrow commercially and the economy remains extremely vulnerable to any further shock, such as a sharp drop in petroleum prices.

In the absence of significant policy changes by the Egyptian government or major new economic windfalls, the longer-term outlook is not encouraging. The government continues to balk at more than minimal economic reform measures, emphasizing primarily measures designed to satisfy consumption and promote short-term stability. Reforms will only be implemented if Mubarak can be convinced that the risks of not moving ahead on them outweigh the risks of doing so.

The symptoms of trouble are abundant. Despite rigid price controls and subsidies, inflation remains at about 13 percent. Consumer imports are expanding as rapidly or more rapidly than foreign exchange earnings. Food imports now equal 50 percent of total food consumption. Egypt's population, now 47 million, continues to grow at a rate of one million every ten months (3.0 percent annually).

Economic growth has not been balanced, but rather has been highly dependent on a few sectors which may not grow as fast as before and which generate very little employment. For example, the current soft oil market, along with falling prices and growing domestic consumption, will slow the growth of foreign exchange earnings from oil exports even in the face of healthy production increases. Indeed, in the past year there already have been signs that the government has become increasingly hard pressed to meet its foreign exchange obligation.

Unless forced to by circumstances, Mubarak is not likely to put political focus on economic problems. Instead, he will probably continue to concentrate on internal and external security. Increased defense expenditures from Egypt's own resources will add to the budget deficit and, if already scarce foreign exchange reserves are used, feed the liquidity problem. In these circumstances,

Mubarak could face some tough choices soon, such as:

- tightening controls on imports;
- reaching an agreement with the IMF on access to the Fund's resources; or
- making foreign policy adjustments which might secure renewed official assistance from Arab oil-producing states.

None of these choices is attractive. Restricting the import of basic food commodities is politically unthinkable. Restricting luxury imports would be insufficient to deal with the problem. Restricting the import of intermediate goods (construction materials, for example) would be economically unsound. The government so far has vigorously resisted IMF conditions for access to the Fund's resources: further devaluation of the Egyptian pound and action to close the gap between domestic and international energy prices. Departures in foreign policy could upset Egypt's relations with the United States and Israel.

Mubarak's experience is weakest in the economic field. Unlike Sadat, he presumably has few preconceived ideas about how to manage the economy and thus will rely heavily on advisors. But, for Egypt, the best economic advice is almost always politically hazardous. Here, we would expect Mubarak to err on the side of caution. We doubt that he will abandon his halting approach to economic reform until he has exhausted all other options.

8.10 THE BALANCING ACT. Egypt's economic planners face an agonizing dilemma: the reforms needed to consolidate Egypt's economic renaissance and promote long-term growth necessarily will continue to foster discontent and political unrest. The Egyptian man-on-the-street sees only a poorer quality of bread or a higher price per loaf. He does not anticipate, nor does he appreciate, price stability in the future. Thus, the government must walk an extremely fine line as it attempts to implement indispensable economic reforms without triggering the political instability which would make reform impossible.

Egyptian vulnerability to destabilizing economic forces was best demonstrated by the January 1977 food subsidy riots which severely shook the government. For a few days there was some doubt as to the outcome. In the end, the government survived and may have learned some lessons that make it less vulnerable today. Importantly, the point was driven home that the economy is Egypt's area of greatest weakness.

III. ECONOMIC ANALYSIS

1.
SUMMARY CONCLUSIONS

1.1 RESOURCES. Oil has played an increasingly important role in Egypt's economy, accounting for a significant portion of export revenue. Water from the Nile is a major resource. On the other hand, arable land is severely limited, with little possibility of expansion through reclamation. Egypt is wealthy in natural gas and minerals.

1.2 RECENT ECONOMIC DEVELOPMENTS. The growing current account deficit necessitated the introduction of emergency reforms, which have proved fairly successful. At the same time, the government has announced an amibitious development plan. Its objectives enjoy the wholehearted approval of international experts, but some are skeptical about implementation.

1.3 DIRECTION OF POLICY. The Open Door Policy did not attract major foreign investment funds. Internationalization of the economy resulted in escalating prices and the intensification of pressures on Egypt's ailing infrastructure. President Mubarak, however, has given no indication that he intends to abandon this policy. His approach is cautious; many question his resolve.

1.4 MACROECONOMIC DEVELOPMENTS. Economic growth has been moderate in real terms, but impressive in the context of worldwide recession. Inflation, reduced through the slowdown of monetary expansion, still remains high.

1.5 SECTORAL DEVELOPMENTS. The oil sector has grown rapidly, although world market conditions have slowed that growth. Future growth may be higher. Agricultural growth has been sluggish and is likely to remain so. Industrial growth will be moderate in view of infrastructural and managerial constraints. The service and distribution sectors have grown rapidly, despite slow growth worldwide; their share of GDP will almost certainly increase. Construction has suffered from slow growth; lower growth in residential construction is likely to keep the growth of the entire sector low.

1.6 BALANCE OF PAYMENTS. The improvement in Egypt's balance of payments due to increased revenue from oil exports, the export of invisibles and foreign aid, was reversed in the early eighties. The transitory nature of these sources of foreign exchange has been amply demonstrated. In the short run, it is likely that Egypt's export earnings will continue to rise. However, the import bill is also likely to grow rapidly. If aid continues at present levels, the capital account is likely to be favorable, insuring a reasonable overall balance of payments.

1.7 FINANCIAL SECTOR. Monetary growth has been curbed, so inflation should abate somewhat. Budget deficits continue to be a serious problem. This requires major structural reforms, especially in taxes (which must be made more elastic) and food subsidies (which must be brought under control). If the government is successful in carrying out the reforms outlined in its current plan, then bank financing of the deficit can be reduced, easing inflationary pressures.

2.
MACRO-ECONOMIC ANALYSIS

2.1 THE PRE-LIBERALIZATION ECONOMY. The performance of the Egyptian economy in the past thirty years has been uneven. The 1952 Revolution coincided with a downturn in the business cycle following the Korean Boom. The October 1973 war coincided with the 'oil price revolution' which opened up new opportunities for investment and development in Egypt. It also triggered a phase of recession combined with inflation in the world economy with adverse repercussions on developing countries, Egypt included.

The decade 1955-1965 witnessed fairly rapid and sustained economic growth as well as a major structural transformation of the economy. Industry and services increased both their output and employment shares. Within industry, there were changes in the composition of output in favor of intermediate goods and consumer durables. The transition from a relatively free, private-enterprise system to a system largely characterized by state planning, public ownership of modern means of production, and wide-range administrative control and policy interference with the economy occurred at this time.

The period 1965-1973 saw a steady decline in the rate of economic growth, with a marked fall in both the rate of investment and domestic savings. Though the decline in economic growth was slowed in the late 1960s, there were no dramatic improvements or signs of sustainable recovery. The economy was suffering from a multitude of problems: distortive economic policies which failed to push up the rate of savings in line with the rate of investment; the impact of the Yemen and Arab-Israeli wars of 1962, 1967 and 1973, and the correspondingly heavy defense burden; the inefficiencies of the public sector and the maladministration of prices, foreign trade and investment programs; and the cumulative effects of the population explosion.

Taking the effects of these two major periods into account, the overall performance of the Egyptian economy as it entered the period of liberalization is fairly clear. Beginning in the early 1950s, Egypt had a ten year period of significant economic growth (1955-1965). Between 1967-73, the economy could not sustain the pace of high economic growth, largely because of the uneconomic diversion of resources to defense and the interruption in aid flows from the west.

Between 1960 and 1973, the GDP (market prices) increased at an average annual rate of about 4 percent. Much of the increase was eroded by the rate of population growth; the per capita income improved only from about LE 65 to LE 100 over this period (at about 2.7 percent a year). The GDP growth rate dropped to less than one percent a year between 1966 and 1973 and there were some years (1966-68, 1972) in which there was actually a fall in real per capita income.

Considering the three major sectors — agriculture, industry and services — a familiar picture emerges. Because of the differential rates of growth between agriculture and industry, the pattern of structural change involved a rapid decline of the share of agriculture in GDP. In the 1950s, industry increased its share of real GDP at the expense of both agriculture and the services. In the 1960s, the rapid growth of the services sector overshadowed that of industry. Egypt has not reached that stage of economic development which is characterized by a decline in secondary relative to tertiary activities. The observed decline in Egypt is, in fact, a sign of economic problems — arising from the population explosion, the indiscriminate expansion of education, and the unsatisfactory performance of agriculture and industry — rather than of economic achievement.

2.2 THE OPEN DOOR POLICY. In the context of the changed economic and political situation following the October War of 1973, the principles of a new economic strategy were put forth in President Sadat's "October Working Paper." It was recognized that in order to accelerate economic growth, changes were required in the roles of the different sectors, public vis-a-vis private, and domestic vis-a-vis foreign. The continuing importance of the public sector was stressed, but it was also acknowledged that the public sector had annexed certain activities that should have remained in the private sector. Hence, new emphasis was given to the desirability of increasing the inflow of foreign investment and technology through an "outward looking" foreign policy.

The initial experience of this new Open Door Policy was not altogether positive. Politically and socially it posed serious internal problems. Private investment, foreign and domestic, was not readily forthcoming. When it did come, it sought access to the domestic market and concentrated on relatively short-term, quick "turn around" situations that were highly profitable and avoided risk exposure. In spite of initial setbacks, the economic recovery initiated in 1974 was sustained and substantial vitality returned to the Egyptian economy. The GDP growth rate which had averaged around 4 percent annually between 1967 and 1974 increased to an annual average of over 13 percent between 1975 and 1978. Liberalization permitted a sufficient degree of flexibility to make adjustments in the operation of the economy. However, fundamental reform in the basic economic policies of Egypt remained elusive, and by 1978 there were signs that the economy's growth was, once again, slowing.

The fiscal situation, after improving for two consecutive years, again deteriorated in 1978 and 1979. In 1980, more than half of the overall deficit had to be bank financed, contributing a roughly 30 percent increase to the money supply. Fiscal 1981 and 1982 showed comparable increases in money supply: 43 percent and 35 percent respectively. Thus, extensive liquidity in the economy and government deficit spending contributed to an accelerating rate of inflation.

On the external side, the balance of payments continued to show strength and improvement with a small deficit on current accounts through 1980. Oil exports, worker remittances, and Suez Canal revenues remained the big elements in this vastly improved situation. Capital inflows for 1981, mostly from foreign assistance and foreign private investment, exceeded $2 billion. Even so, in the latter part of 1981, events — the assassination of Sadat, a troubled world economy, the "oil glut," and a high and growing level of imports — placed Egypt in severe straits in its foreign exchange balances. Worker remittances and tourism receipts fell sharply and Canal and oil earnings fell far short of expectations (although they did register modest growth). Declining exports and rising imports led to a 30 percent increase (over the 1980 level) in the trade deficit, ballooning to over $5 billion. The government deficit again rose sharply to cover the rising costs of subsidized goods and growing imports of foodstuffs.

The Open Door Policy is still operative although serious reconsideration of some of its basic tenets has been occasioned by the negative impact liberalization is having on the rate of inflation and income distribution. The dominant role in the economy will in any case remain with the public sector. Public and private sector investment expenditure reached an estimated 24 percent of the GDP in 1979 compared to only 15 percent prior to 1974. Total investment for 1980/81 was 4 billion Egyptian pounds ($5.72 billion); the public sector accounted for over 85 percent of this sum.

2.3 STATE OF THE ECONOMY 1978-1983. The Egyptian economy continues to undergo the structural transformation initiated in 1974. Official estimates place growth of the GDP in 1978 at about 8.0 percent, 9.7 percent in 1979, and approximately 9.2 percent in 1980/81.

National Accounts

National Accounts	Amount 80/81 (million US $)	Annual growth rates 1978	1979	1980/81 (est)
Gross Domestic Product (GDP)	24,233.0	8.0	9.7	9.2
Agriculture	4,901.0	5.5	4.2	4.3
Industry	4,154.0	10.6	8.4	7.9
Petroleum	4,440.0	22.0	10.3	18.9
Services	9,640.0	6.3	12.7	10.6

The growth of all sectors has abated in recent years, as, indeed, has overall GDP growth. The growth of the oil sector has been erratic, reflecting pricing changes and corresponding revenue modification. The industrial sector has grown faster than agriculture. This has tended to reduce the relative importance of agricultural output as a percentage of GDP (down to 20 percent in 1981/82). At the same time, industrial output accounted for 14 percent of GDP in 1981/82, with the service sector accounting for 18 percent (lower than in the mid-seventies) and the distribution sector accounting for 27 percent (higher than in the mid-seventies).

Bank financing of budget deficits has exacerbated inflationary pressures by increasing the growth rate of the money supply. The inflation rate in 1979 was placed at 30-40 percent, which continued into first quarter 1980; government actions in the latter part of the year brought it under control. Inflation has officially been estimated at 11.1 percent in 1980/81, 16 percent in 1981/82 and 15.8 percent in 1982/83.

Current Account
(million US $)

	80/81	81/82	82/83
Exports	4,050	4,102	3,854
Petroleum & petroleum products	2,922	2,922	2,654
Imports	-8,722	-8,574	-8,400
(Merchandise balance	-4,672	-4,472	-4,546)
Net services and transfers	3,401	2,416	3,140
Suez Canal	870	909	970
Tourism	712	611	600
Remittances from abroad	2,855	2,032	3,100
Current account	-1,271	-2,056	-1,406

On the external side, the balance of payments continues to show strength and improvement with a smaller deficit on current account in 1982/83. (The 1981/82 current account deficit figure has recently been officially revised to $2.116 billion, while the estimate for 1982/83 has been officially revised to -$1.733 billion; the ameliorating trend remains evident.) Oil exports, worker remittances, and Suez Canal revenues remain the big elements in this vastly improved situation. Capital inflows for 1984, mostly from foreign assistance and foreign private investment, are projected to be well in excess of $2 billion.

2.4 EFFECTS OF LIBERALIZATION: 1973-1983. The change of strategy, prompted by a complex set of internal and external, political and economic factors, coincided with a significant change in Egypt's international political position accompanied by new hopes for a lasting peace. Egypt, as a centrally located and traditionally leading Arab country, with a large and relatively skilled population, sensed the opportunity for an important and unique role in a period of booming growth and trade in the oil producing Middle East. This change in the external environment made redirection of economic strategy towards more open and world market oriented policies seemingly more palatable and likely to succeed in rapid fashion. Moreover, in its turn toward the west (primarily the United States) for resolution of the Arab-Israeli conflict, it was felt that an economic commitment to the political initiative was required. Thus, the redirection of economic policy was seen as complementary to the new choices being made on the foreign policy front.

Liberalization was not conceived of as a radical break with past economic philosophy or economic priorities. There was some shift of emphasis and a series of cumulative changes in policies that finally amounted to a major change, but all within a framework of continuity and, in particular, with a continued commitment to the social achievements of the 1952 Revolution. In spite of the low level of per capita income and tight resource constraints, Egypt has developed a strong commitment to a kind of welfare state and the state is perceived and perceives itself as directly responsible for the welfare of the Egyptian people. Liberalization in Egypt does not and cannot imply the withdrawal of the state from active intervention or the regulation of the economy by market forces alone. Therefore, resource mobilization and rationalization of domestic policies and prices must be achieved within a framework that is politically and socially viable.

So far, the new president, Hosni Mubarak, has not been in a position to change economic policy. If anything, he has proven very indecisive. With respect to revising and redirecting the Open Door policy, he had to conclude that the economy has been burdened with a new set of problems for which solutions must be sought. However, the politics (both domestic and international) of preserving a liberal atmosphere while engaging in more forceful action to elicit responsible behavior from the private sector most assuredly induced caution on President Mubarak's part.

In the longer term, Mubarak might be in a position to undertake more basic economic reform. Much will depend upon the degree to which he finds himself hostage to the political methods of the Sadat regime or able to place sufficient distance between himself and that regime to purposefully rationalize the Egyptian economy. In the event that the latter is the case, he will nevertheless have to divine a role for the public sector consistent with fulfilling the social obligations of the state begun under Nasser.

Although liberalization did not proceed in the vein which was anticipated, it has, nevertheless, had a significant impact on the Egyptian economy. The table below indicates the transformation from a "level," largely stagnant economy, to a more "open," trade and external capital flows dependent economy.

Trade and Capital Flow Impact on the Egyptian Economy

	Percentage shares in GDP	
	1972/1973	1979/1980
Exports (goods and services)	14.6	43.8
Imports (goods and services)	21.0	53.0
Gross Annual Foreign Capital Flow	10.4	17.6
Total Stock of MLT Debt Outstanding and Disbursed	38.0	58.0
Debt Service (% of GDP)	2.4	8.2
(% of Exports)	16.2	21.4
Investment	22.3	30.4
Private Investment	5.2	9.4
Average Annual GDP Growth (Constant Prices)	8.0	

Aid flows from the Arab states (discontinued after the peace with Israel) and the west have risen dramatically, increasing Egypt's debt sharply. Similar dramatic increases have been registered on the investment front. After 1975, total gross investment (including stock accumulation) has averaged 30 percent of GDP. Private investment has almost doubled as a share of GDP, with direct foreign investment largely responsible for this change. Public investment also continued to grow relative to GDP. The overall growth of GDP reflects at least in part the high investment rates, averaging about 8.0 percent since 1972/73.

Private sector investment, while increasing substantially, has not **significantly** affected the overall public sector-private sector balance in total fixed investment and contribution to total production.

3.
DEVELOPMENT PLANNING AND PUBLIC POLICY

3.1 CURRENT DEVELOPMENT STRATEGY AND DEVELOPMENT ISSUES.
To provide for the needs of its growing population, Egypt has devised an economic growth strategy which can produce yearly growth rates of 8 percent. In the Egyptian context, such a high growth rate can come only from industrialization aimed at import substitution, production for export markets, and creation of infrastructure which stimulates the introduction of technology that increases productivity. A development strategy based in large part on technological modernization will enhance the use of several potential development advantages available for Egypt's economic growth: in human resources, favorable market position, and a large, relatively well-advanced resource and industrial base. These potentials for development will not be fully realized unless large investments are made, foreign technologies are imported and adapted, the rate of technological innovation is increased, and structural changes are made in economic planning, the system for resource allocation, and the management of public enterprises.

3.2 THE 1982-86 PLAN. A new four-year plan was announced for 1982/83 to 1986/87. It is generally recognized that Egypt has not had a serious planning effort since the 1960-65 Plan. The highly unstable character of the region and the domestic and external difficulties stemming from this made effective long-term planning virtually impossible. The current planning mode (although not officially stated as such) is to use an annual rolling plan formulated within a longer-term planning framework. Given the relatively short-term character of many of the economic policies of the government, this approach to planning is probably the most practical. Typically, Egyptian development plans have embodied rather unrealistic growth projections based on investment levels that could not be generated or sustained. Also, these plans have failed to juxtapose appropriately the issue of current consumption versus future growth. The new plan has, however, received cautious praise from international experts, who see it as a thorough re-evaluation of the country's development strategy in view of recent developments, embodying more mature (if still ambitious) objectives in the form of a package of far-reaching adjustments.

3.3 OBJECTIVES OF THE PLAN. The plan identifies the following constraints to Egypt's development strategy: an output structure biased toward non-commodity production; an overburdened infrastructure; high current account deficits; excessive dependency on service exports and transfers; high budget deficits and excessive monetary expansion; an inefficient public sector pricing policy; inadequate managerial capacity in both public and private sectors. This formulation is seen by some as a direct response to pressures from the international community. To overcome these constraints, the plan proposes:

– a high level of economic growth
– a higher rate of national savings
– development of commodity-producing sectors
– supporting infrastructural development
– developing human resources
– correcting persistent balance of payment deficits
– proper public sector pricing policies and effective management

In terms of macroeconomic targets, the plan still calls for GDP growth of 8.6 percent (at market prices), with industry growing at an average 9.5 percent annually, and agriculture 3.7 percent – higher than in the recent past. Savings and investments are projected to rise as a proportion of GDP: savings are projected to grow to 24 percent of GDP in 1986/87 from 12 percent in 1981/82, thus lowering the percentage of investment to be financed by foreign savings and allowing the current account deficit to drop from 10 percent of GDP to 2 percent. In consequence, GDP consumed will fall from 88 percent to 77 percent. The external debt is to grow very slowly, from LE 13 billion to LE 16 billion in 86/87 ($18.59 to $22.88 billion), and the external debt ratio to decline to 21 percent from 24 percent. Exports should grow at 10.5 percent faster than GDP (8.1 percent at factor cost), which in turn will grow faster than imports (4.3 percent). Public consumption will grow faster than private consumption while private investment will grow as a proportion of total to 23 percent (from 18 percent in the recent past).

Experts have noted that these are highly ambitious goals, which may not all be realistic. The plan has been criticized for not outlining specific policies to reach these goals in much detail. Nonetheless, the goals are formulated in a manner calculated to please Egypt's international financial backers, who regard these goals, even if only partially successful, as moving Egypt toward a sustained development path.

3.4 HUMAN RESOURCE DEVELOPMENT POLICY. Since 1973, the attempt to restructure the economy in order to induce a more rapid pace of modernization has met with limited success. At the core of the issue of technology transfer is the formulation of a sound human resource development strategy. People are the major asset of the Egyptian economy and it is only in their efficient organization and utilization that greater efficiency in the utilization of more scarce resources (capital, foreign exchange, land) can be forthcoming.

Just as in the case of a technology policy and, more broadly, an economic development policy, there is not at present a cogent and well-conceived human resource development policy. In essence, the three areas — technology, economic development, and human resource development — are inextricably linked in the case of Egypt, and the manpower question is clearly key.

There are three major factors which indicate that a reorientation of the country's development strategy emphasizing the development of human capital would make a significant contribution to the solution of Egypt's medium and long-term social and economic problems.

First, it is recognized that, despite the relatively successful performance in the 1970s, Egypt's long-term structural problems remain. The main issue results from the fact that Egypt's recent growth and balance of payments performance has depended on such <u>external</u> factors as oil exports, worker remittances, Suez Canal revenues, and foreign aid, and not on domestic production, particularly in industry and agriculture. There are serious uncertainties about the future prospects of these external factors, which involve risks for the country if it continues to depend upon them. As a consequence, a safer road to the future would and should lie in the development of domestic resources in commodity-producing sectors and on exports of these commodities, complemented by effective import substitution.

Second, in the Egyptian context, utilization, upgrading and development of human resources should be a focal point of development policies. The relative shortage in certain segments of the labor market caused by large-scale labor migration to neighboring Arab countries should not lead to undue optimism, since the country's endemic problems of employment, e.g. unemployment, rigidities in the labor market, and maladjustments, continue to persist. These problems are bound to be magnified given the structural characteristics of the population, namely the massive growth of the labor force, increasing labor force participation rates, urbanization, increasing educational levels and therefore expectations. Furthermore, the present pattern of growth is not conducive to domestic employment creation. Thus, in the present setting, even moderate declines in investment growth and exports could quickly reverse the gains achieved in the recent past.

Third, the social contract between the government and the people of Egypt, which has for decades contributed to social stability, may be difficult to maintain without increasing utilization and generation of domestic resources, and particularly without the participation of the people in the process of development. The government may face difficulties to meet its rapidly increasing social obligations because of resource constraints. Measures such as subsidies, employment guarantees, wage policies, and protective controls have already exceeded economically affordable limits. Under the present circumstances these measures have also become factors which cause misallocation and misutilization of resources, and therefore slow down the growth of the domestic productive base. It is therefore both necessary and reasonable to ask people to contribute to the production of goods and services under the conditions of the social contract.

3.5 INDUSTRIAL SECTOR. In the long run the industrial sector will have to provide the basis for employment expansion and rapid growth. In view of its large domestic market, adequate natural and human resources, and key geographic position, Egypt can pursue industrial development policies combining efficient import substitution with export promotion. The major question is how to redirect investments to achieve this.

There are a number of projects in the current investment program which have not been carefully prepared and evaluated. The large and particularly capital-intensive projects in the present investment program require analysis of their impact on capital and human resource utilization.

Appropriate pricing of capital and choice of technology are important issues. The possibilities for substitution between capital and labor are critical in determining the expansion of employment in different sectors. In the Egyptian case, agriculture, construction, and to some extent trade and services, are sectors offering such possibilities, whereas in other sectors, substitution between labor and capital has a limited scope. For sectors with limited substitution possibility, employment generation in the long term will be determined by the level of investment. For agriculture and construction, in most cases, investment tends to be a substitute for employment (mechanization of certain activities in agriculture; heavy equipment and prefabrication in construction). More careful analysis is needed on the dimension of technological choice in investment programming.

The development of Egypt's project preparation and evaluation capacity, and building a sizeable stock of well evaluated projects, are major tasks. This is important for reasons related to efficient sector development as well as adequate choice of technology responding to both employment and competitiveness criteria.

3.6 AGRICULTURAL SECTOR Development of the agricultural sector poses a different set of issues for human resource utilization. The major question is "has agriculture in Egypt reached its limits?" The question cannot be adequately answered without appropriate analysis of the impact of current policies which appear to have distorted both the behavior and the performance of the agricultural system.

The dominant element related to policies affecting agriculture has been the extraction of surpluses from this sector to promote development of other sectors of the economy and to promote a program of public subsidies for urban consumers. This policy and the contradictory and conflicting signals given to producers have resulted in:

- encouraging shifts in cropping patterns, mostly counter to Egypt's comparative cost advantage;
- eroding both the means and incentives for increasing output and productivity in major crops, on-farm investment and adoption of technological change;
- creating conditions for out-migration from the

sector, thus distorting both the employment and wage structure.

It is equally important to know the impact of present policies and to make assumptions about how the system would have performed in the absence of these policies and how it would have responded to well conceived measures.

In terms of physical environment (sun, soil, and water), Egypt's agricultural potential should be very promising. Despite the land constraint, this potential can be exploited more effective by:

- moving from low-value added to high value-added crops;
- more intensive cropping;
- increasing yield in basic crops;
- preservation of agricultural land area.

This approach would require the upgrading of the agricultural labor force. Within this framework there are possibilities for technological choice responding to human objectives. For example, mechanization, although essential and useful when replacing animal power for performance of certain activities (e.g. pumps replacing animals to raise water), may have moderate or high labor-substitution effects in other areas (e.g. tractors replacing bullocks and labor in land preparation, and threshing machines replacing labor in harvesting).

3.7 LABOR MIGRATION POLICIES. Labor migration represents another major dimension of the human resource utilization issue as it relates to the technology transfer question. Here, as in other aspects of development policy, insufficient thought has been given to the specific impacts on the economy that a highly generalized migration policy might have.

Egypt has a very liberal policy encouraging migration of its labor force, particularly to neighboring Arab countries; the Constitution treats migration as a civil right. The profound effect of migration on the Egyptian labor market makes an active policy in this area a necessary part of any employment strategy. However, employment considerations alone have not sufficed for formulating a sound comprehensive migration policy. Such a policy should cover Egypt's political and cultural as well as economic objectives in exporting manpower to the region.

The migration policy does not, at present, involve selective encouragement or discouragement of different categories of the labor force. In cases where migration drains Egypt's high-level and limited-skill resources, financial disincentives to migration should be considered. For unskilled labor, and underemployed categories of government employees, active measures can be taken to stimulate migration. There is also the need to ensure adequate inflow and use of remittances. Migrant labor can be given incentives as well as active support for channeling remittances into areas which the government considers desirable.

At the present time, there is a lack of knowledge about the magnitude and pattern of migration and a total absence of clear perception of the prospects for the future. This is a serious shortcoming, since any unexpected serious change in the dimensions and pattern would have dramatic consequences for the Egyptian society and economy. The drain on the highly skilled categories of workers has had obvious deleterious effects on the Egyptian economy, particularly in such areas as construction, maintenance and repair of equipment and machinery, and the operation of sophisticated plant (computer-based production, electric and telecommunication services, modern hospital equipment, etc.). Remittances pose an off-set to these adverse effects, but there has been no attempt to calculate the actual opportunity cost to the economy of unlimited and unstructured labor migration.

3.8 RECENT ECONOMIC POLICIES. Inflation and income distribution continue to pose serious difficulties for the Egyptian leadership. The economy performed reasonably well in 1978 and 1979. In 1980, real GDP growth was on the order of 8-9 percent. President Sadat, concerned about the slow pace of the revitalization of the economy, assumed a more direct role in steering the future course of economic development in May 1980.

There were a number of immediate policy objectives pursued under the new management arrangement: an improved pattern of income distribution; the achievement of greater social equity through raising the wages of fixed-income groups; freezing prices on the commodities consumed by lower-income groups; and re-evaluating the Open Door Policy to reduce the likelihood of additional negative impacts on the rate of inflation and income distribution. To achieve these objectives, the following was announced:

- the minimum wage for the public and private sectors has been increased by 25 percent to LE 20 ($28.60) per month;
- all taxes for defense and national security have been cancelled;
- the public sector wage scale is to be revised to allow higher pay for college graduates;
- electricity rates for consumers will be reduced;
- the prices for 300 commodities produced by public sector companies will be reduced;
- farmers will receive higher payments on certain agricultural commodities.

Additional measures have been taken to achieve greater social equity including more extensive use of economic tools beyond fiscal policy. Other recent measures include:

- revision of the customs tariff structure which reduces duties on many consumer items and restructures rates to stimulate investment;
- rationalizing the own-exchange import system by redirecting funds through the domestic banking system and raising the costs of importing luxury items;
- mobilizing the resources of the domestic banking system for longer term uses by requiring that 15 percent of foreign currency deposits be placed in interest-bearing accounts in the Central Bank;
- raising the interest rate for LE deposits to mobilize more domestic savings.

3.9 CONSEQUENCES OF RECENT POLICIES. At the beginning of 1981, the Egyptian economy remained a curious mixture of temporary strength and continuing weakness. The underlying elements leading to this schizophrenia in the character of the economy were to be found in the difference between current internal and external economic performance.

The external economic situation showed continuing strength. Revenues from the sale of oil were declining somewhat. Worker remittances had increased as had the revenues from the widened Suez Canal and tourism. In 1980, balance of payments performance was sufficiently improved that Egypt recorded its lowest deficit, $800 million, in almost a decade. Capital inflows from foreign assistance, and in a more minor way, private investment, had further added to the accumulation of foreign exchange reserves.

Cumulatively, these external economic resources generated $9.1 billion in 1980. However, the warning signs were already apparent and the continued buoyancy of the economy, dependent as it was upon potentially unstable and temporary phenomena largely external to Egypt, carried with it a high degree of vulnerability. It was unwise for the government to interpret these transitory phenomena as representative of solid improvement in the internal capacities of the economy to generate sufficient resources for long-term growth. While it clearly served to ease the immediate pressures for policy change, the question remained: What are the prospects for economic policy reform that could set the economy on the proper track for the coming decades?

By the end of 1981, the Egyptian economy was under considerable pressure as a result of low current account receipts, structural imbalances, and mismanagement. The national budget deficit was LE 4.7 billion ($6.72 billion) in 1981/82. Major causes contributing to the deficit were:

— plummeting oil revenues due to lower prices;
— shortfall in Suez Canal revenues, a record $900 million in 1981 but still far short of the $1.5 billion hoped for after widening the canal;
— an inelastic, slow-growing tax system, relying on specific rather than ad valorem taxes;
— open-ended expenditure commitments, such as ever-escalating direct subsidy costs (estimated at $2.3 billion, or 31 percent of total budget revenue in 1981/82) to ensure a fixed market price for basic foodstuffs; implicit subsidies on oil products (domestically priced in Egypt at 7-77 percent of their import prices); and in the pricing policies of the public sector, where output price rigidity creates a drain on government funds;
— salary increases of 30 percent, deemed politically necessary, for public sector workers.

By mid-1982, the ameliorating trend in Egypt's balance of payments appears to have ended. The current account registered a deficit of $2.056 billion (by some estimates as high as $3.5 billion, the magnitude being a function of the month when 81/82 is regarded to have begun), 62 percent higher than the previous year. The underlying causes of Egypt's deteriorating balance of payments position included:

— declining oil revenues and Canal shortfall;

- workers' remittances 29 percent below their 1980/81 level;
- low revenue from tourism (no more than $611 million for fiscal 1981/82);
- the price of cotton, Egypt's major cash crop, approximately 20 percent lower than the previous year;
- imports, maintained at a high level in excess of $8 billion as a result of fiscal and monetary expansion in 1981.

3.10 EMERGENCY REFORMS. The situation was improved as a result of emergency reform measures which were passed in fiscal 1981/82. These included:

- curbing imports, especially of consumer goods;
- liberalizing terms which banks offer workers sending remittances from abroad;
- curbing growth of public expenditures (current and capital);
- tightening domestic credit.

These measures made possible significant improvement in the balance of payments situation, with the current account deficit narrowing to $1.4 billion, and the overall balance of payments showing a surplus, allowing Egypt to reduce short-term debt and build reserves. The fiscal situation also improved, but the public sector deficit remained large (21 percent of GDP in 1982/83 compared with 24 percent in 1981/82). The growth in the money supply decelerated noticeably, but still remained high at 20 percent annually (for money and quasi-money combined) for the second quarter of 1983.

3.11 GENERAL EVALUATION. Despite persistent structural imbalances and a reactive approach to policy formulation, there are several factors about Egypt's economy which justify a degree of optimism, namely:

- Egypt's debt service ratio continues to fall, so it encounters few difficulties borrowing abroad. Egypt has negotiated a $200 million loan with Chase Manhattan.
- As Egypt's relations with the Arab world improve, it will trade on larger scale with Arab countries.
- Arab financial institutions are interested in dealing with Egypt.

– In curbing consumption and imports and expanding Egyptian participation in development, President Murabak is supported by broad sections of the population, including some who had been hostile to his predecessor's Open Door Policy.

This optimism must, however, be conditioned by analysis of the prospects for real economic reform. Without such reform, there can be little optimism regarding the future capability of the economy to generate internally the resources required for further economic development.

The overriding concern with respect to policy change of any significance has to do with the potential for political instability that might follow. Implicit in this concern and occasionally stated by Egyptian officials is the belief that past government policies, while possibly deficient in purely technical terms, have nevertheless provided an atmosphere of political stability. From such reasoning it follows that perceived political reaction to any attempt to change present policies is sufficient to offset the inclination to do so, even if one accepts the argument that the long-run benefits to the economy would be substantial. The events of January 1977, when civil violence broke out as a result of the government's attempt to reduce consumer subsidies, is often cited in this regard.

Egypt's economic problems remain considerable, and will require years of reform to solve. In the short run, Egypt is certain to encounter severe – but not insuperable – budget and balance of payments problems. Egypt has fairly good financial standing internationally. American support represents huge amounts of aid (although the Egyptians are beginning to resent the restrictions and slow disbursement). It enjoys support in international institutions like the IMF and the World Bank, although it has come under pressure from both to control spiraling government spending, especially on food subsidies.

The real choice is up to President Mubarak. Policy in action during his transition period was expected and is occurring. While there is not, as yet, a clear indication of the direction he will ultimately take, it is generally believed that he will continue the transformation of the Egyptian economy begun by Sadat in 1973.

Egypt's resource endowment is deficient in several major respects: it is capital short, its area of inhabitable and arable land severely restricted, and its internal capacity to generate sufficient foreign exchange is limited. It does have considerable human resources, but this is both an advantage and a disadvantage. A rapidly expanding population aggravates other resource limitations without necessarily producing the optimum economic output of having a large, educated pool of manpower.

3.12 TECHNOLOGY. Technology is one of the main factors taken into account in considering applications for investment projects; the prospect of obtaining technology new to Egypt is reason for giving approval. The technology factor, including the cost of importing technology, is assessed in a number of ways, but no adequate and sound methodology has evolved.

Egypt's capacity to absorb technologies effectively can be assumed given the reasonably well-educated state of its human resource base. However, as in other instances where the country has some comparative advantage, deficiencies in development policy and strategy have led to a highly distorted prism through which the process of technology transfer is viewed. Thus, although the 1973 policy of economic liberalization has as one of its major aims the technological modernization of Egyptian industry, it is questionable whether the government has given adequate thought to the "appropriate" vis-a-vis "new" technology question. More effective utilization of Egyptian resource endowments carries with it the need for competent analysis of the choice of technology.

That any consistent reference has been made to the labor versus capital intensive issue — as this relates to the choice of technology — is not apparent in the Egyptian case. Despite the country's relatively low wages and comparatively plentiful supply of labor, there is a propensity to install modern equipment rather than machines of older and less capital-intensive design. For example, the importation of industrial machinery more than three years old is now prohibited by law.

3.13 MEDIUM-TERM PROSPECTS. Economic growth is likely to continue to be moderate. A growth rate at constant factor cost in excess of 6 percent was expected for GDP for the fiscal year 1983. Future economic growth is likely to be in roughly the same neighborhood in the medium term, a performance considered quite respectable relative to what LDC's have been registering during the current worldwide recession. Inflation is likely to remain within a controllable range in view of the moderate growth in money and quasi-money (22 percent annually in the third quarter of 1983). The growth of the previously fast-growing oil sector will shrink to 4.5 percent in 1983/84 (estimated

1982/83 growth was 6 percent). Oil sector growth may increase to 7 or 8 percent in the mid-eighties. The agricultural sector will continue to grow at about 2.5 percent annually, though that growth rate may increase slightly over the next few years as new planning priorities take hold. The industrial sector is too constrained by infrastructural and managerial problems to sustain more than 8 percent growth; 7.5 percent may be a more realistic growth rate for the mid-eighties, planning priorities notwithstanding.

Consumption is likely to continue to increase at annual rates of 5.5-6 percent through the mid-eighties. Public savings could be boosted as a percentage of GDP from 5.4 percent in 1982/83 to nearly 8 percent in 1986/87. Private savings cannot be boosted much in the face of slower economic growth. The private investment-GDP ratio, however, could rise from 7.5 percent in 1982/83 to nearly 10 percent in 1986/87, permitting the public investment ratio to fall from 20 percent in 1982/83 to a couple of percentage points less in 1986/87. This could narrow the public sector's savings deficit and the private sector's savings surplus.

Expanding imports and rising interest payments will more than wipe out the gain from increased export earnings over the next four years; by 1986/87, the current account deficit would nearly double from its 1982/83 estimated level of $2.2 billion. The balance of payments situation could deteriorate as interest and amortization payments on external debt increase. Assuming moderate (and fairly realistic) success in the government's austerity plan, the budget deficit as a percentage of GDP could decline from an estimated 21.5 percent in 1982/83 to 15 or 16 percent in 1986/87, with bank financing of the deficit thereby declining from 7 percent of GDP to as little as 3 percent, thus reducing inflationary pressures.

The debt service ratio is most likely to rise slightly from 25.1 percent of export earning in 1982/83 to a still manageable 27.5 percent in subsequent years.

3.14 EXTERNAL FACTORS. Those who contend that the present character of the Egyptian economy is sufficient to induce political stability but insufficient to generate the increasing resources necessary to maintain this character (in terms of internal capacities) are led to the conclusion that any shortfall must necessarily be covered by resources external to the economy. At the present time, this is precisely what is taking place. It is conceivable that the present circumstances could extend for some time to come, significantly diminishing the need for extensive policy reform. While conceivable, such circumstances would make the nation particularly vulnerable. Should any or all present external sources of funds and foreign exchange earnings begin to diminish, it is doubtful that the economy could absorb the impact effectively and quickly.

Quite aside from the question of whether the extent and very positive character of external factors will be maintained over the long term, there are already several serious and potentially destabilizing domestic issues with which the economy is confronted. Employment, housing, and a more general deterioration in the quality of education, medical care, and transportation services cannot be contained, nor can the present capacity of the internal economy generate sufficient resources to deal with these issues meaningfully. Thus, while it may be correct to argue that indulging in reforms may lead to political instability, it is no less true that failing to do so may lead to the same.

4.
PETROLEUM SECTOR

4.1 SECTOR GROWTH. Egypt's petroleum sector continues to register considerable growth as it did throughout the 1970s. Revenues from petroleum increased four-fold between 1978 and 1980, benefitting from both the sharp price increases and the bringing into production of new fields. From a negligible contribution to the GDP of 1-2 percent at the beginning of the decade to over 13 percent in 1979, this sector recorded a significant 22 percent contribution in 1980 and 15 percent in 1981/82. The contribution to export earnings is equally impressive. Accounting for 37 percent ($0.37 billion) of export revenues in 1978 and 65 percent ($2.5 billion) in 1980, it registered 80 percent ($4.7 billion) in 1981/82 and 78 percent ($4.2 bilion) in 1982/83. Thus, oil exports remain the mainstay of Egyptian export earnings. Traditional exports, primarily cotton, continue to decline in importance.

It is anticipated that in the near term this sector will remain most important to attaining real GDP growth in the neighborhood of 8-10 percent for the economy as a whole. However, the decline in demand in the world oil market has weakened earnings growth. In the first quarter of 1981, Egyptian top-grade crude oil (Suez Blend 33°) was marketed at $40.50 per barrel; by July, this had declined to $33. Worldwide conditions brought about a major price reduction in the winter of 1982/83 (the price had fallen to $27.25 in March, 1983); nearly a quarter of this reduction has since been restored.

The growth of the petroleum sector is significant, and new discoveries have eased somewhat the decline in the rate of growth of crude oil production evident in 1978 and 1979. Production averaged 0.595 mbd in 1980, topping 0.700 mbd late in the year. It averaged 0.635 mbd in 1981 and early 1982. In the first quarter of 1983, crude production stood at 0.667 mbd. No new major discoveries have occurred; hence, long-term growth is still in doubt. While marginal finds have eased the dip in earnings due to price decreases, the "scissors" effect — declining production and rising domestic demand (at subsidized prices) — portends sharply curbed performance of this sector by the mid 1980s.

Refinery Location, Ownership and Capacity (1982)

Site	Company	Capacity (b/d)
Alexandria (Ameriyeh)	El-Nasr Petroleum	50,000
Suez	El-Nasr Petroleum	17,000
Suez	Suez Petroleum Processing	18,000
Tanta	Suez Petroleum Processing	16,000
Musturid	Suez Petroleum Processing	74,000
Alexandria	Alexandria Petroleum Co.	60,000
Total		**235,000**

In the first quarter of 1984, Egypt raised the prices of different grades of Egyptian crude oil twice (by 25 cents in each instance), reflecting a mild improvement in demand for Egyptian oil worldwide. The price of the Suez blend (33°) remained at $28 a barrel throughout that quarter, keeping Egyptian crude more or less in line with OPEC prices, although Egypt is not an OPEC member.

4.2 SHORT-TERM PRODUCTION ADJUSTMENTS. The sharp growth rates in petroleum sector earnings between 1978 and 1981 are not likely to be maintained or repeated. The bringing into production of new finds has altered the situation somewhat in the short term. However, domestic consumption at subsidized prices is increasing at about 12-15 percent per year, a far greater rate than the growth of total production. Unless new major discoveries are made, the amount of oil available for export will continue to decline. In the past, marked increases in world oil prices have helped the government to maintain and even increase earnings. In addition, the government has shown an inclination to pump oil beyond optimal levels to insure this sector's continued contribution to foreign exchange earnings. As prices have now declined significantly, it is difficult to maintain the present earnings level even though average daily crude oil production has risen.

The worst case scenario thus remains one in which future crude production will not increase substantially beyond the 600-700,000 barrels/day range; in result the present export surplus will disappear by late 1984, given the current rate of growth of domestic demand. Barring new discoveries and any major change in domestic price policy, after 1984 Egypt will once again become a net importer of petroleum products with attendant negative effects on its balance of trade position.

OAPEC economists have made definite forecasts about Egypt's energy situation. Assuming modest growth in energy demand (7 percent annually in the 1980s and 5.6 percent in the 1990s), Egypt's demand will be slightly over 50 million toe in the year 2000, with an energy deficit of 11 million toe.

4.3 NATURAL GAS. Important discoveries have been made in natural gas, still an underexploited resource; more is being produced in association with oil than can be currently utilized. Natural gas has potential as a domestic substitute for LPG (in which capacity it is currently being used in some towns). It can also be used as feedstock for fertilizers and other petrochemicals. Currently utilized gas is made available to power stations and industrial installations. Four fertilizer plants using gas as feedstock are already in operation: two at Talkha, one at el-Dekheila, and one at Suez.

Major fields include Abu Madi in the Delta (on stream since October 1974), Abu Qir near Alexandria (offshore), and Abu Gharadiq in the Western Desert. There are plans to expand output, especially at Abu Qir, and to use more associated gas from the Gulf of Suez fields (a station is projected at Ras Bakr for that purpose).

Production and Distribution of Petroleum, Natural Gas, and Petroleum Products
(millions of metric tons)

	1975	1979	1980/81	1981/82	1982/83
Total Output of Crude Petroleum	11.7	26.3	31.0	32.5	34.4
Foreign Companies	2.9	5.6	5.4	6.0	6.8
Egyptian	8.8	20.7	25.6	26.5	27.6
Used for Refining[a]	10.0	12.5	15.1	14.9	16.9
Net Exports	2.4	8.4	10.5	11.6	10.7
Domestic Consumption of Refined Products	7.4	9.9	11.7	12.7	15.1
Production[c]	8.6	11.4	13.4	14.5	16.4
Net Exports	1.2	1.5	1.7	1.8	1.3
Natural Gas Output	N.A.	0.9	1.8	1.9	2.2

[a] Difference reflects refining losses & changes in stocks.
[b] Derived residually and includes changes in stocks.
[c] Preliminary estimates.

5. INDUSTRY

5.1 SLUGGISH OVERALL GROWTH. The Egyptian government continues to view the country's long-term development prospects in terms of its ability to industrialize rapidly, absorbing the anticipated large increase in the labor force and off-setting rising food import requirements by increasing export of manufactured goods. While the real growth rate of the industrial sector has been substantially higher than the agricultural sector over the past fifteen years, the industrial sector nevertheless continues to suffer from a series of problems, many of a long-standing nature. The new members of the labor force for the next fifteen years are already born and the continuing weakness of the country's industrialization strategy will have potentially serious consequences.

In recent years, real sector growth has been approximately 5-6 percent. The rate of growth of the sub-sectors has varied widely with beverages, fertilizers, cars, tractors and trucks, and steel registering relatively higher growth than textiles (yarns and fabrics), phosphates, and processed foods. Sector growth has already slowed, falling well below the projected 7.5 percent for 1979 and leveling off at near 6 percent. Industry accounted for nearly 14 percent of GDP in 1981/82.

The improvement in industrial sector performance from 1974-1978 was due largely to increased utilization of existing productive capacity rather than increased capital investment. The real growth of imports of capital and intermediate goods declined, in part due to continuing inconsistencies in tariff policy, and these in large measure accounted for the present slowdown in sector growth. Future growth will be dependent upon a marked increase in the rate of capital investment.

5.2 FUTURE GROWTH DEPENDENT UPON MAJOR ECONOMIC REFORMS. The efficiency factor remains the key and dominant issue in the public enterprise sector. Operating 110 enterprises, the government's policy of consumer subsidization and the vague requirements of establishing social justice hamper rationalization of public sector performance. The effort to stimulate public sector performance by a revitalization of the private sector and joint ventures between public sector companies and foreign multi-national corporations (MNCs) has not had any significant effect. In 1973 the public sector accounted for approximately 75 percent of total industrial output and 90 percent of fixed capital investment. In 1979 the private sector accounted for $1.8 billion out of $5.7 billion total industrial production, or 30 percent. The public sector remained the largest investor, still accounting for 90 percent of total fixed capital investment.

Recently, the government has reaffirmed that the public sector is to remain dominant in future economic growth strategy. Public sector enterprises continue to operate under severe burdens and remain ill-prepared to take advantage of the Open Door policy. Legislation pertaining to public sector operations is undergoing major revision and may, ultimately, ease the constraints. However, the continuation of price controls given rapidly rising input costs, inadequate investment budgets, excessive employment levels, and an inappropriate wage structure will clearly hamper rationalization of this sector's performance. Investment in manufacturing weakened in 1979 and again in 1980, and the public sector continues to operate at a considerable disadvantage when compared to the nascent but growing private industry sector.

It is not anticipated that the government policy of liberalization will have any significant effect on industrial sector growth in the absence of major economic reform. The private sector, until recently, was showing an increased inclination to make medium- and long-term investment in industrial projects. The quality of these products has not, as a rule, been as high as the government would like. Rather, private projects have tended to take advantage of existing distortions in the economy and the inefficiency of the public sector. To redirect private sector initiatives, the government has promulgated new regulations, the primary intent of which is to stem private sector speculation. Business confidence has been shaken to some extent; however, the longer-term intent and impact of these new rules is not clear at this time.

5.3 REDUCED LABOR MIGRATION AND GROWING POPULATION. The declining budgets of the oil-rich Arab countries is clearly impacting on the demand for Egyptian labor.

Reductions in demand and the current rate of 400,000 new entrants per year to the domestic labor force in Egypt will put great pressure on the government to industrialize more rapidly. The agricultural sector cannot absorb much more labor and it will fall to the industrial sector to create the needed capacity for employment opportunities. Unless the government is willing to permit further redundancy by overemploying in its public sector companies, an unattractive option, it is clear that dramatic and rapid modernization of the industrial sector using appropriate technology is paramount.

6.
AGRICULTURAL SECTOR

6.1 LOW GROWTH. With the exception of 1978, which proved to be an unusually good year in Egyptian agriculture, with real growth reaching 3 percent, the long-term growth trend of agricultural output has been low, averaging 1-1.5 percent per year for the past several decades. In recent years, the area under cultivation for two of the main crops, cotton and rice, has fallen. However, yields of both crops have increased significantly (31 and 5 percent respectively for 1978 and 1979), and since have fluctuated; in 1981/82, their yields were 52.1 percent and 3.5 percent above the 1974/75 level.

Two other basic crops, wheat and maize, have had relatively stable production records. Wheat yields have been stable while the total area planted has increased by about 14 percent since 1978. Both yield and crop area for maize have increased somewhat, 8 and 6 percent respectively since 1978.

Other important crops include millet, sugarcane, groundnuts and onions. Fruits and vegetables have been growing in importance because of price distortion owing to selective subsidization and the possibility of large-scale exports at international prices. Citrus fruit production, in particular, has grown rapidly; in 1981/82 it was 44 percent higher than the previous year.

6.2 POLICY PROBLEMS. Although Egypt can, in any given year, experience relatively improved performance in its agricultural production, such improvement cannot be viewed as a long-term phenomenon. Any fundamental change in the performance of this sector remains hampered by government policies on investment, pricing of agricultural output, and procurement procedures for agricultural inputs. The disparity between relative prices for agricultural commodities and the prices for non-agricultural goods remains sufficiently significant to deter any new initiatives.

Although the sector is not taxed directly, one estimate indicates that the rate of implicit taxation ensuing from the artificially low prices for output and the policy of partial or complete procurement of crops at these fixed prices is about 30 percent. The government does provide a number of inputs at subsidized prices; however, these do not provide marked relief from the effects of government policies, nor do they serve to offset the current rate of implicit taxation.

Selective subsidization has also led to effective price distortion, discouraging the cultivation of vital crops (such as wheat) and promoting the cultivation of cash crops, mainly fruits and vegetables. This has not only aggravated Egypt's food-production problems; it has also led to escalating fruit and vegetable prices and increased trade in these crops has pushed domestic prices closer to international levels.

6.3 TECHNOLOGICAL PROBLEMS. At present, the agricultural sector accounts for about 20 percent of the GDP and about 40 percent of total employment. Its importance has been declining steadily, which is more or less consistent with the government's development policy emphasizing industrialization. It is anticipated that the low growth trend and relative stagnation of this sector will continue, as will the government policies currently in effect. Serious technical problems could serve to reduce this sector's contribution to the economy further. Rising salt levels, due to the extensive irrigation made possible by the construction of the Aswan High Dam and the deterioration of the drainage system, may begin to erode yield levels. The government has extensive land reclamation schemes in effect or under construction, but the costs involved are prohibitive.

Finally, increasing urbanization takes place at the expense of arable land although, ostensibly, law prohibits this. The result is that high-yield Delta land is taken out of production and, if replaced, is replaced with reclaimed land that is often marginal in quality and productive capacity. The overall projection, therefore, is for continuation of current low growth trends.

7.
MANPOWER

7.1 EMPLOYMENT EFFECTS OF LIBERALIZATION. Egypt is well endowed with human resources. It is one of the most highly populated countries in the Middle East and lies at about the median for rate of population growth. The sustained increase in economic activity has been instrumental in improving the domestic employment situation. The continued demand for Egyptian labor throughout the Middle East, resulting in the employment abroad of 800,000 Egyptians, has added to this trend.

The leading employment sectors are agriculture (46 percent), services (16 percent), manufacturing (15 percent), and commerce (11 percent). Historically, the most rapid expansion in employment has occurred in the construction sector. Employment in manufacturing has grown almost as rapidly but not all of this growth is considered productive. The third growth sector is commerce. Increases in employment in commerce have been more rapid in recent years due to the policy of trade liberalization initiated in 1974. Employment in agriculture peaked in 1971, and has since begun a gradual decline.

Public sector employment has risen dramatically in the past two decades, accounting for over 34 percent of total employment in 1978. This growth is, in the main, attributable to the following factors: selective guaranteed employment policies in the government; social and political pressures for employment stemming from rapid population growth; the growing importance of central planning, ownership, and administration of the bulk of economy.

7.2 CONTINUING PROBLEM AREAS. In 1981/82, the total labor force included about 11.5 million workers, or about 26 percent of the total population. In addition, 1,667,000 Egyptians were estimated to be living abroad in 1982, of whom slightly over half a million are believed to be workers. The labor force is generally considered well-educated, with an adequate mix of skills and capabilities.

Shortages exist and, on occasion, these can severely hamper the progress of development projects dependent upon skill categories in short supply. Such shortages (technicians, mechanics, and construction labor) are affected by external demand and inherent weaknesses in the educational structure. Other problem issues in the area of manpower include an imbalance of labor supply and demand due to the government's guaranteed employment policy and government pay and promotion practices; unstructured and uncontrolled labor migration that draws critical skills abroad; and high illiteracy and dropout rates, despite government policies aimed at reducing these handicaps.

Projected real growth rates in the main employment sectors do not appear to be of sufficient magnitude to absorb the additions to the labor force anticipated in the next few years. The demand for Egyptian workers abroad has begun to slow, and it does not appear feasible to view this as a future substantial outlet for new entrants to the labor force. The continuing commitment to provide an informal program of unemployment insurance through public sector employment and the continued weakness in the internal economy may mean that the government will be faced with new pressures to provide employment, irrespective of negative economic consequences.

Inflation is causing more women and children to enter the formal and informal labor force. Rising agricultural wages (15-20 percent annual increases since 1978) and high demand for casual labor have led to shortages in the labor supply with a corresponding increased availability of jobs for women, particularly in the public sector. There are indications that school dropout rates are considerable.

7.3 REDUCED MIGRATION CREATES NEW PROBLEMS. The declining revenues of the oil-rich Arab countries will create new difficulties for Egyptian authorities. Falling levels of remittances will be only one dimension of the strain resulting from this new phenomenon; if the government cannot find the means to absorb returning workers and new entrants to the labor market, political destabilization might well result.

The only prospect for absorbing increased labor supply is for the economy to be put on a solid growth footing. This requires purposeful reform of the economy which, so far, has not appeared to be possible given internal and external political conditions. However, in what now may prove to be a Hobson's choice, the government must come to recognize that preserving the policy status quo cannot forestall the prospect of political disturbances arising from increasing unemployment.

Percentage Distribution of Workers
By Economic Sectors

Year	Agric.	Indust.	Oil	Elect.	Constr.	Services
1965	51.4	11.3	N/A	0.2	4.7	32.4
1970	48.9	11.0	N/A	0.3	4.7	35.1
1975	43.8	12.1	0.2	0.4	4.7	38.8
1980	36.6	12.5	0.2	0.5	5.9	44.3

8. CONSTRUCTION SECTOR

8.1 ROLE IN DEVELOPMENT STRATEGY. The construction sector is relatively small in terms of its contribution to the GDP (approximately 5 percent) and employment (6 percent). However, this sector plays a critical role in implementing major aspects of the government's development strategy, emphasizing as it does major investment and housing projects.

This sector has traditionally comprised a substantial component of investment, with construction input requirements averaging 43 percent of total investment. Construction input requirement ratios range from 32.5 percent for non-metallic product investments to 99 percent for housing construction projects. Historically, for the Aswan High Dam, for the basic metals and public utilities sectors, and for a variety of services, the ratio has been in excess of 50 percent. Hence, the interrelationships of the construction sector (in providing intermediate inputs to other sectors and in receiving those inputs from other sectors) represent key elements in the Egyptian economic development equation.

Among the major construction projects being executed in Egypt is the Cairo Metro scheme. Work on the project, which will cost an estimated $200 million, was begun in 1982 with French financing, its object being to relieve traffic problems in Cairo. The project has since become the focus of considerable controversy, and technical delays (caused by inadequate charting and water seepage) have caused work on the project to be viewed as a major impediment to traffic rather than as an aid. Work is now expected to be finished in 1987, at which point an estimated 60,000 passengers an hour will be able to travel along the 43-kilometer line between 33 stations.

8.2 BOOM TAXING CAPACITY. The current construction boom is taxing this sector's capacity to serve the substantial demands placed on it. Foreign employment opportunities have reduced the labor available, and periodic shortages of construction materials hamper the ability of the sector to meet these demands. It is anticipated that the current high rate of non-residential construction will abate somewhat over the next few years. However, the demand for new housing construction will increase sharply, especially given the government's increased emphasis on housing in the new Five Year Plan.

Investment in the construction sector has proved the most volatile of all sectors. In 1979, it increased to LE 160 million ($228.8 million) from LE 132 million ($188.76 million) during the previous year. In 1980/81, it fell to LE 129 million ($184/47 million). In 1981/82, investment rose to LE 152 million ($217.32 million).

In the housing sector, investment has been increasing sharply, from LE 128 million ($183.04 million) in 1977 to LE 581 million ($930.83 million) in 1981/82.

9. FINANCE SECTOR

9.1 INCREASING LIQUIDITY AND HIGH INFLATION. One of the most significant economic developments in 1979 (which has continued, although in abated form, into the first half of 1983) has to do with the increasing liquidity in the Egyptian economy and the effects of this factor on prices and output. Despite attempts to increase domestic resource mobilization, the structure of public finances remains unchanged from previous years. As a result, Egyptian government accounts remain highly vulnerable to inflationary pressures. Outlays continue to grow far more rapidly than revenues, leading to further government borrowing from the domestic banking system and an acceleration in the growth of the money supply.

Through the 1970s, the money supply is estimated to have grown at an annual average rate of 21 percent while the GDP in current and constant prices increased at 15 and 7 percent respectively. Quasi-money (non-current deposits) grew at an even faster rate, about 28 percent annually, and total liquidity averaged a rate of growth of 23 percent per year. First quarter 1983 results indicate that the rate of growth of total liquidity has picked up considerable momentum; annualized, it would represent an increase of 33 percent over 1979.

In 1981, money and quasi-money combined grew at a rate of 43 percent. For 1982, the rate was 35 percent. Some fiscal austerity measures and pressure from the international community reduced the rate to nearly 20 percent in the first quarter of 1983. It has barely increased since (22 percent in the third quarter of 1983).

Estimates on the rate of inflation vary considerably. Consumer price index information in Egypt serves at best as an approximate guide. Thus, interpretations of various observers currently range up to 30 percent. Irrespective of the precise dimension of the current rate of inflation, one theme is relatively common: prices are rising and the rate at which they are rising continues to accelerate.

Fiscal Summary
(billion LE)

	1980/81	1981/82	Estimated 1982/83
Public Revenues			
of which: Taxes	7.4	8.2	9.4
Other	(4.2)	(4.7)	(5.7)
Public Expenditures	10.6	12.9	14.5
of which:			
Current Expenditures & Capital Transfers	(4.6)	(6.0)	(7.7)
Subsidies	(2.2)	(2.2)	(2.0)
Investment	(3.8)	(4.7)	(4.8)
Public Sector Deficit	3.2	4.7	5.1
Source of Financing:			
External	(1.1)	(1.2)	(1.5)
Domestic, Non-Bank	(1.2)	(1.3)	(1.9)
Banking Sector	(0.9)	(2.2)	(1.7)

The general explanation for the large price increases is the growth in money supply and non-current deposits at rates far in excess of the growth in real output. At the end of 1979, the economy was already very liquid (by international and historical Egyptian standards). Only if the government succeeds in controlling public spending (as it has shown promise of doing, albeit to a very modest degree) can the current rate of monetary expansion be prevented from accelerating further.

9.2 MEASURES TO STEM INFLATION. The Egyptian government has relied on a number of monetary measures to reduce consumption. However, these measures have done little to stem inflation. Some success was registered when the government raised interest rates on domestic savings, bringing them more into line with internationally available rates. The continuing high rate of inflation has eroded the value of the Egyptian pound, re-establishing the case for sterner policy measures.

The precise direction which the government can or will take to deal with inflation, should it begin to reach crisis proportions, is not evident. Present policy is short-term, will most probably lead to additions to already existing inflationary pressures, and will not serve to reduce political pressures growing out of increasing dissatisfaction with price movements.

9.3 PROSPECTS FOR PUBLIC FINANCE. If plans to bring subsidies (especially on food items) under control prove successful, spending on subsidies could be reduced to 6 percent of GDP in 1986/87 (from an estimated 8.3 percent in 1982/83). Assuming no reduction in current government expenditure but no great increase, some reduction in public fixed investment, and little change in the percentage of GDP taxed over the same period (a likely prospect), the overall deficit could be reduced to 15 or 16 percent of GDP in 1986/87 (from an estimated 21.3 percent in 1982/83). This could reduce financing from foreign savings somewhat, but more significantly it would reduce bank financing sharply from an estimated 7 percent of GDP in 1982/83 to nearly 3.5 percent in 1986/87, thus curbing a primary driving force for inflation.

9.4 BANKS. At the end of 1983, three new national banks had begun operating (in the provinces), in addition to the Bank of Hong Kong. This brought the total number of commercial banks up to 39, including four public sector banks, 34 privately and jointly owned banks, and the Faisal Islamic Bank, which operates under a separate charter. Bank assets grew at 19.8 percent in 1983. The fastest growing assets were bank loans to other banks (31.4 percent growth). Deposits grew at 16.2 percent. Deposits were distributed thus: 32.7 percent held by the public sector; 49.4 percent by households, 15.8 percent by the private sector, and 1.1 percent by others.

9.5 INCREASED POWERS FOR THE CENTRAL BANK. A minor banking scandal occurred in early 1984 when three banks were involved in dealings with a money changer and trader who obtained credit through illegal use of post-dated checks, which subsequently proved to be unauthorized by the issuing bank and therefore invalid. This led to the enaction of legislation tightening the control exercised by the Central Bank of Egypt over the activities of commercial banks in Egypt. The new regulations entail the following:

- the Central Bank of Egypt (CBE) may now set credit ceilings for banks violating its guidelines;

ceilings for banks violating its guidelines;
- the CBE may appoint supervisory members of the board for such banks;
- a credit ceiling of 25 percent of paid-up capital plus reserves is in effect for any single customer (except for government agencies and public sector institutions);
- the CBE can now veto all appointments (including past ones) to bank boards.

These decrees have greatly increased the CBE's ability to enforce its guidelines (previously it could sanction a bank only by taking the drastic — and destabilizing — step of revoking its license). The membership of the CBE's own board has also been broadened to encompass more than the four publicly-owned banks which previously dominated it.

9.6 ISLAMIC BANKING. Islamic banking has proved remarkably successful in Egypt. Faisal Islamic bank, which opened in 1977, has expanded dramatically; its net profits are projected to be in excess of $134 million. The Pyramids Bank, in serious difficulties because of unauthorized dealings in post-dated checks which resulted in the bank's insolvency, is being taken over by the Al-Baraka Investment and Development Company, a burgeoning Islamic banking group based in Jeddah.

10.
OTHER SECTORS OF IMPORTANCE

10.1 DISTRIBUTION AND SERVICE SECTORS. Given the heavy investments being made in infrastructure, the growth rate in the distribution sector has been, and will continue to be, quite high. Estimated 1982/83 growth is 8.5 percent, down from 9.9 percent in the previous year.

Investments in transportation and communication and the Suez Canal, and a large increase in the number of commercial and financial institutions, are spurring growth. Economic liberalization has been particularly beneficial to growth in these sectors.

Growth in the service sectors was estimated at 8.6 percent in 1982/83, down from 9.8 percent in the previous year. Major investments in utilities, tourist facilities, and housing are projected over the next few years. This should permit sustained growth in these sectors.

10.2 TOURISM. The general liberalization in the exchange and trade systems and in international travel procedures led Egyptian authorities to develop the tourist industry; most measures focused on the encouragement of private sector investment (both domestic and foreign) in hotels and other tourist facilities through tax and other incentives, greater attention to the improvement of existing facilties and services, upgrading the skill levels of tourist personnel, and generally improving the management of public sector tourist facilities.

Attracted by these developments and by improved profitability of hotels (where occupancy ratios have been above 90 percent with little seasonal variation in recent years), investment in the tourism sector has risen dramatically. However, actual expansion of tourist facilities has lagged behind demand, and the rise in tourist earnings continues to be hampered by inadequacy of facilities and services; for example, there are only 5,500 deluxe and first class hotel rooms in Egypt (about 9,000 if second class hotels are included). Tourist arrivals in Egypt rose rapidly after 1974, but the growth appears to have decelerated since 1977.

Tourist revenues showed a marked increase in 1981, rising from $780 million to over $1 billion. Total tourist nights in 1980 were up 20 percent over 1979. However, the twin blow of Sadat's assassination and the growing gap between the official and free market exchange rates, resulting in tourists changing a greater volume of funds through unofficial channels, drove tourist receipts down in 1981 and 1982. Tourist receipts were $611 million in 1981/82, $600 million in 1982/83. In 1981/82, there were 1.36 million tourist arrivals and 9.6 million tourist nights spent.

11.
FOREIGN TRADE

11.1 OVERALL SITUATION. Through 1980, Egypt experienced steady improvement in its balance of payments (BOP). Exchange earnings from petroleum ($1.5 billion in 1979) and worker remittances ($2.2 billion in 1979) are largely responsible for this trend. The current account deficit in 1979 remained below $1.3 billion, as had been the case in 1978, and dropped to about half that figure in 1980. Owing to the decline in earnings from the oil exports, the export of services, and in transfers, which became evident in 1981, the current account deficit began growing, reaching a peak ($3.5 billion by some estimates) in 1981/82, but shrinking thereafter because of corrective measures (latest semi-official estimate of the 1982/83 current account deficit, is $1.4 billion, which some experts believe is too conservative by a third).

Placed in a long-term perspective, analysis of trade performance indicates several important trends. The trade import surplus declined moderately from 1975 through 1977, then increased sharply in 1978 and again in 1979. Imports grew at about 10 percent annually up to 1978, subsequently accelerated markedly — 17 percent in 1978, 24 percent in 1979, 14 percent in 1980, 12 percent in 1981. Foreign exchange constraints and government measures caused the growth rate to drop to nearly zero in 1981/82, and to be slightly negative in 1982/83.

Commodity exports in the 1976-78 period drifted upwards. The increase in the 1979 export level was a significant 25 percent, and in 1980 a massive 53 percent, mainly due to oil exports. There followed a period of negligible or slightly negative growth (1981-83), mainly due to shrinking revenue from oil exports. Exports other than oil have fallen consistently since 1974, though they seem to have stabilized at a level near $1.2 billion in the past four years.

11.2 SOURCE OF SHORT-LIVED CURRENT STRENGTH. The balance of payments continued to be fairly robust through 1983, the worst estimate of the 1982/83 current account deficit being in the neighborhood of $2.2 billion. Net capital inflows from foreign aid, direct foreign investment, and loans offset this deficit, the only serious strain on the capital account being debt service. Total amortization of official and private debt was a modest $1.4 billion in 1982/83, though the amount will certainly increase after 1985. The major weakness in the BOP situation is that the sources of strength – oil, remittances, and Canal and tourist revenues – have proven transitory. Non-oil exports have performed poorly in recent years while imports continue to increase at a rapid rate. Estimates of imports in constant prices show that imports of intermediate and producer goods declined by about 12-13 percent in 1979 over 1978. Conversely, imports of consumer durables (in constant prices) increased by over 15 percent as did imports of basic foodstuffs such as wheat and flour. A large import surplus, comprised mainly of intermediate and capital goods, has one implication for the future development of the economy while a large surplus to finance the import of consumer goods has another, and more worrisome, implication. The fact is that, in the past few years, the import surplus has been heavily dominated by consumer goods. Of equal concern, but of unknown quantitative dimension, is the possible negative impact of debt repayment schedules that will have to be met in the course of the 1980s. Amortization payments could be nearly double the present level in 1986/87.

In 1980, imports showed extremely rapid growth with food and other consumables accounting for over 35 percent of total imports. Population growth and rising incomes have led to significant increases in consumption with no corresponding offset by increased domestic production. The openness of the economy has prompted increased imports of luxury goods, including manufactured goods. Import growth has seemingly been brought under control by corrective measures in the past two to three years. Imports of capital and intermediate goods have continued to grow in relative importance.

11.3 RECENT ESTIMATES. Recent official estimates of the 1982/83 balance of payment figures (accompanied by slightly revised 1981/82 estimates) indicate a smaller current account deficit in 1982/83 ($1,733 million), compared with $2,116 million in 1981/82. The preliminary figures for the first half of 1983/84 indicate a deficit of $365 million for the six-month period, some 40 percent lower than the $604 million over the corresponding period of fiscal 1982/83. This has encouraged observers to conclude that the government's goal of $1.500 billion for the fiscal 1983/84 deficit is quite feasible.

The improvement in the current account situation thus far in 1983/84 was largely due to the increase in remittances from abroad, which rose by 43 percent to $1.716 billion in the first half of 1983/84. This reflects steadily improving terms for transfers from abroad; the announcement of a new incentive rate in April 1984 (LE=89 cents) for foreign transfers is expected to enhance remittances channelled legally (not through the black market) further.

While the overall picture shows a definite improvement, there is less cause for rejoicing about the transfer and service balance other than remittances. In particular, tourism and miscellaneous revenues declined by 18 percent in the first half of 1983/84 (reflecting continued recession world-wide, notably in Europe). Suez Canal revenue increased by a miniscule 3 per cent, reflecting the slump in international shipping and the inability of the Canal to provide passage for supertankers at a time when smaller tankers are becoming uneconomical. A further slump can be expected if the recently reported mining of the Red Sea endangers Canal shipping to the point of raising insurance premiums.

The trade deficit has definitely deteriorated (but not enough to cancel the overall improvement in the transfer and service balance, the other component of the current account). While imports increased by a modest 3 percent in the first six months of 1983/84, and non-oil (mostly agricultural) exports increased by 26 percent, the 15 percent decline in the value of oil exports to $1.110 billion has caused the trade deficit to increase 7 percent to $2.230 billion for the first half of 1983/84. Oil export decline was a result of lower prices, which have been slightly raised in the first quarter of 1984, and of rising domestic demand for oil, spurred by the still artificially low domestic prices of most fuels.

11.4 PROSPECTS. Income from tourism should rise steadily, possibly exceeding $900 million in 1986/87. Suez Canal revenue should also rise (as the world recovery restimulates trade and renovation work bears fruit) to $1.5 billion or more in 1986/87 — barring serious disruptions in trade or a dramatic increase in insurance premiums. Oil income will increase as production is maintained at high levels, but the dollar amount will depend on international market conditions. Non-oil commodity exports, especially those of agricultural goods, should increase substantially with government encouragement, to over $2 billion in 1986/87 (estimated 1982/83 figure is $1.2 billion). Worker remittances should continue to grow (barring unusually severe restrictions on Egyptian labor abroad, or major labor repatriation), wage inflation and continued (or improved) liberal terms of transfer at home could bring about an increase of remittance to $4 billion in 1986/87. Thus, total earnings from exports of goods and services should rise from $11.5 billion to as much as $18 billion in 1986/87.

Imports will register considerable growth over the same period. Food imports will continue to rise, reflecting shortages and government priorities. Imports of needed intermediate and capital goods will show substantial increases according to plan. Even with continued curbs, imports of manufactured goods should rise by 50 percent or more in the next four years because of technological changes and the open nature of the economy. Thus total merchandise imports should increase from an estimated $9.8 billion in 1982/83 to nearly $16 billion in 1986/87.

A major factor in determining Egypt's balance of payments situation will be the future of official transfers, primarily from the United States. Foreign aid from the United States stood at approximately $2.325 billion for fiscal 1984. Of that, $1.375 billion was for military sales ($465 million in grants and $910 million in loans). An estimated $250 million was given as food aid. Aid dispensed through the Economic Support Fund ($750 million in fiscal 1984) is administered by U.S. AID. The manner in which U.S. AID funds are administered has aroused considerable resentment in Egypt. An enormous number of projects initiated under the program (over 2,000) have stagnated with no perceptible result; U.S. AID has almost never authorized release of funds in those dead-end projects for alternative uses. In addition, data gathering by U.S. AID officials for project evaluation has aroused considerable suspicion in view of close American ties with Israel.

For 1985, the U.S. government has proposed a slightly reduced allocation of $2.170 billion: $1.175 billion for military sales, $243.3 million for food aid, and about $750 million through the Economic Support Fund. It appears likely that, despite American reluctance to continue aid on a massive scale with little to show for it and despite strong Egyptian criticism of U.S. AID,

American aid to Egypt will continue unabated for some time. The United States remains desirous of maintaining close ties with Egypt, and the Egyptian government needs to be able to point to continued American aid to justify its pro-American policy.

Balance of Payments Summary
(billion US $)

	1980/81	1981/82	Estimated 1982/83
Exports of goods/services	11.1	10.4	11.5
of which: oil	3.2	3.3	2.8
remittances	2.9	1.9	2.9
Imports of goods/services	-13.5	-13.9	-13.7
of which: merchandise	-10.3	-10.4	-9.8
Current account balance	-2.3	-3.5	-2.2
Medium/long-term			
capital flows	2.3	2.3	2.4
Unallocated	-0.1	0.6	0.7
Overall balance	**-0.2**	**-0.6**	**0.9**

12.
FOREIGN BUSINESS OUTLOOK

12.1 FOREIGN PRIVATE INVESTMENT. The policy of economic liberalization has entered its eleventh year. Foreign private investment was to serve as the pivotal element in the transformation of the Egyptian economy, in particular, of the public enterprise sector. Generally, the policy of liberalization had more success in permitting the revitalization of the Egyptian private sector than it has had in attracting large-scale foreign investment. Foreign investors are attracted to strong, disciplined economies; new policies, not just new laws, are required if the Egyptian economy is to be attractive. Basic policy change being rejected, foreign investment has not met the target initially envisaged.

By 1981, $1.6 billion in projects in the private sector had been approved. The pattern of investors seeking approval but not actually moving to implementation, established early on under the Open Door Policy, remains a common feature of private sector behavior.

In 1982/83, inflows of direct foreign investment are believed to be in the range of $1.4 billion, representing only a 5.5 percent increase from 1981/82, and a decline from the 1979 high of $1.5 billion.

12.2 IMPACT OF LIBERALIZATION. In many respects, liberalization has come too quickly to the Egyptian scene. Large parts of the economy, which have been sheltered and run inefficiently for too long, suffered from the abrupt exposure to private sector competition. Liberalization has contributed to inflation and, more seriously, to the emergence of disparities in the distribution of income.

The government continues to reflect upon its experience with liberalization. The social tensions created by conspicuous consumption, the rapid rise in prices, and the growing concern that the public sector has not and may not benefit in the manner envisioned at the outset, have induced re-examination of liberalization policy.

12.3 CHANGES IN EXCHANGE SYSTEM. In 1981, the Ministry of Economy announced changes in the exchange system. These changes were designed to decrease the demand for dollars and strengthen the Egyptian pound. In conjunction with the changes designed to close the gap between the official and free market rates for the dollar, an import licensing system is operative. It is designed to regulate demand for hard currency and reduce imports of luxury goods. While initially envisioned as a means to stabilize the exchange market, the new system is also to be used to restrict imports of raw materials and intermediate imports.

These changes have had an unsettling effect on the private business community. The government has indicated that it is not departing from liberalism in the economy. However, businessmen feel that these new rules signal a broader policy reversal.

12.4 SHORT-TERM OPPORTUNITIES. As far as U.S. business is concerned, short-term opportunities are perhaps most attractive to suppliers. Egyptian imports of U.S. goods and services exceeded $2 billion in 1981, and this figure will continue to rise. Foreign exchange availability, a critical concern in the past, is once again a possible constraint. The continued heavy flow of U.S. aid provides substantial opportunities for financing U.S. goods and services. Virtually all U.S. AID programs are restricted to U.S. source procurement.

12.5 LONGER-TERM CAUTION. With respect to the longer term, selected investment opportunities may be attractive although caution should be exercised. The potential volatility in the economy always carries with it the prospect of policy change. Making a long-term commitment, possibly involving substantial capital outlays, must await more precise government articulation of the future direction of liberalization of the economy. Some medium-term investments are being made and the revitalization of Egyptian capitalism, if it continues, means that there will be a growing local base of expertise with which U.S. firms might interact. Careful and continuing analysis of the situation is merited if the potential investor feels that profitable opportunities exist in the Egyptian market.

12.6 U.S. INVESTMENT DISAPPOINTING. Apart from the petroleum sector, both the Egyptian and U.S. governments have been disappointed that U.S. investment has not been greater. As of 1981, only about $40 million had been invested in Egypt by U.S. firms. There are several reasons why U.S. firms have chosen to remain on the sidelines. Most U.S. firms are unacquainted with business methods in the Middle East. Firms are either not flexible enough or not interested sufficiently in the opportunities in Egypt to take the implicit or explicit risks involved. European firms, often more experienced in dealing in the region, fare better as a group, but only marginally.

There are U.S. firms that have shown determination to enter the Egyptian market, but they are frequently discouraged by the bureaucratic hurdles that must be overcome before operations can begin. While it was hoped that the reorganization of the government in May 1980 would lead to greater coordination among government ministries, improvement has been slow. Ambiguity continues to exist between Egypt's announced support of an Open Door policy designed to liberalize its economic system, and its commitment to protecting public sector firms which are heavily subsidized and controlled by the government. Impediments to inflows of foreign capital may be reduced if legal liberalization plans succeed, making public sector companies more competitive with Law 43 firms.

IV. EGYPT: STATISTICAL APPENDIX

Table 1.

BASIC INFORMATION

Official name: Arab Republic of Egypt (Jumhouriyyat Misr al-Arabiyya)

Country Abbreviation: EY

Date of Independence: February 28, 1922

National Flag: Tricolor (red, white, and black) of three equal horizontal stripes with the national emblem in the central white stripe.

National Emblem: A stylized, upright eagle, usually black in color, facing forward with wings partly raised and its beak turned to its own left. On its chest the stripes of the flag are vertically displayed and in its claws is a scroll with the words in Arabic script, "Arab Republic of Egypt."

National Anthem: "To Thee, To Thee, My Country, I give My Love and My Heart"

National Holidays: July 23   National Day: Revolution Day
                        June 8   Evacuation Day
                        December 27   Victory Day

Also, variable Islamic festivals and the Coptic festival, Sham al-Nasim. The Nile Flood Festival is an unofficial holiday.

Weights and Measures: Both metric and traditional systems are used. The main traditional units are:

1 metric Qantar: 50 kg	1 Kadah: 1,717 liters
1 Qantar: 157.50 kg	1 Ardeb: Varies from 120 to 155 kg
1 Rotl: 0.45 kg	1 Keila: 13.7 liters
1 Dirhem: 3 gr	1 Rob: 6.86 liters
1 Oke: 1.24 kg	1 Feddan: 4,200.8 sq m
1 Heml: 249.6 kg	1 Kassabah: 12.60 sq m

Currency Units: Egyptian pound (LE)

Languages: Arabic, English

Geographic Facts

Area: 997,738 sq km
Bodies of Water: Lake Nasser, Nile River
Capital City: Cairo   Population: 5,074,016

Nature of Government: Democratic socialist

Date of Constitution: September 11, 1971

Foreign Policy Position: Pro-Western

Past Leaders:

Farouk	Apr 1936 to July 1952
Mohammed Neguib	June 1953 to Nov 1954
Gamal Abdel Nasser	Nov 1954 to Sept 1970
Anwar al-Sadat	Sept 1970 to Oct 6, 1981

Diplomatic Representation:

U.S. Ambassador in Cairo: Nicholas A. Veliotes
Egyptian Ambassador in Washington, D.C.: Abdel-Raouf el-Reedy
Egyptian Ambassador to the UN: Mr. Ahmed Khalil

Membership in Regional Organisations:

Arab Bank for Economic Development
Arab Fund for Economic and Social Development
Arab Monetary Fund
Economic Commission for Africa
Islamic Development Bank
Organization of African Unity
Organization of Arab Petroleum Exporting Countries
Organization of the Islamic Conference (suspended May 1979, restored 1984)

Membership in International Organizations:

Economic Commission for Western Asia
United Nations
International Bank for
    Reconstruction & Development
International Development Association
International Finance Corporation
International Monetary Fund
United Nations Development Program
United Nation General Assembly
United Nations Relief & Works Agency for
    Palestine Refugees in the Near East
World Bank

Table 2.

CABINET LIST (July 1984)

Head of State....................................President Hosni Mubarak
Prime Minister..Kamal Hassan Ali
Deputy Prime Minister, Defense &
  Military Production....................Field Marshal Muhammad Abdel-
Deputy Prime Minister,
  Minister of State for Education
  & Scientific Research...........................Mustafa Kamal Hilmi
Minister of Foreign Affairs.....................Ahmad Ismat Abdel-Majd
Minister of Petroleum
  & Mineral Wealth..........................Abdel-Hadi Muhammad Qandil
Minister of Finance..................................Salah el-Din Hamed
Social Insurance, Minister of
  State for Social Affairs...................................Amal Osman
Construction, Minister of State for
  Housing, Public Utilities.........................Abdel-Fattah Sidqi
Justice...Ahmad Mamdouh Atai
Transport, Communications & Naval
  Transport....................................SuleimanM etwalli Suleiman
Culture...................................Muhammad Abdel-Hamid Radwan
Irrigation....................................Isam Radi Abdel-Hamid Radi
Electricity & Energy...........................Muhammad Maher Abaza
Supply & Interior Trade..........................Muhammad Nagi-Shatla
Cabinet Affairs, Minister of State
  for Administrative Development.............Atif Muhammad Muhammad Abid
Planning and International Cooperation..........Kamal Ahmad el-Ganzouri
Industry............................Muhammad Mahmud Faraj Abdel-Wahhab
Interior..Ahmad Rushdi
Economy & External Trade.........................Mustafa Kamal el-Said
Tourism & Civil Aviation.........................Muhammad Wagih Shandi
Education & Instruction...........Abdel-Salem Abdel-Kader Abdel-Ghaffar
Local Government............................Hassan Suleiman Abu-Basha

MINISTERS OF STATE

Immigration Affairs & Egyptians Abroad............Albert Barsoum Salama
Foreign Affairs......................................Butros Butros Ghali
Manpower & Vocational Training................Saad Muhammad Ahmad
People's Assembly & Shoura Affairs...................Tawfiq Abd-Ismail
Military Production..........................Gamal el-Din Ibrahim
Health...Muhammad Sabri Zaki
Information................................Muhammad Safwat el-Sherif
Agriculture & Food Security.................................Yusif Wali
Awqaf (Relgious Endowments)...................Muhammad Ahmad Abu el-Nur

Table 3.

EGYPTIAN POLITICAL GROUPS

Political Group	Leader	Position
National Democratic Party (NDP)	Muhammad Rashwan (sec. gen. Cairo)	center
New Wafd Party (NWP)	Fuad Sarageddin	center-right
Ikhwan (allied with NWP in May 1984 elections)	Omer al-Telmisani	Islamic traditional
Unionist Progressive Party (UPP)	Khaled Mohieddin (sec. gen.)	left
Umma Party (UP)	Ahmad al-Sabahi	traditional religious
Liberal Socialist Party (LSP)	Mustapha Kamel Murad	right-wing
Socialist Labour Party (SLP)	Ibrahim Shukri	center-left
Communist Party (outlawed)		left

Table 4.

RECENT MAY 1984 NATIONAL ASSEMBLY ELECTION RESULTS *

Competing Party	Popular Vote	%	Assembly Seats
National Democratic (NDP)	3,856,372	72.9	390
New Wafd and Muslim Brotherhood (NWP)	798,550	15.1	58
Socialist Labor Party (SLP)	372,385	7.04	
Unionist Progressive Party (UPP)	220,673	4.17	
Liberal Socialist Party (LSP)	35,761	0.67	
Total	5,283,741		448

* Election turnout was 41.87%. 8% of vote was necesary to obtain representation in the assembly. Thirty-one assembly seats are guaranteed to women and are appointed, i.e., they belong to the NDP.

DEFENSE

Table 5.

MILITARY EQUIPMENT AND PERSONNEL

Army: 315,000 (180,000 conscripts).

2 Army HQ.
3 armored divisions (each with 1 armored, 2 mechanized brigades)
5 mechanized infantry divisions (each with 2 mechanized, 1 armored brigades)
3 infantry divisions (each with 2 infantry, 1 mechanized brigades)
2 Republican Guard Brigades
2 independent armored brigades
9 independent infantry brigades
2 airmobile, 1 parachute brigades
12 artillery brigades
2 heavy mortar brigades
6 anti-tank guided weapon brigades
7 commando groups
2 surface-to-surface missile regiments (1 with FROG-7, 1 with Scud B)
Armored fighting vehicles: 860 T-54/-55, 200 M-77, 600 T-62, 250 Am-60 (M-60A3) main battle tanks; 30 PT-76 light tanks; 300 BRDM-1/-2 scout cars; 200 BMP-1 mechanized infantry combat vehicles; 2,500 OT-62, BTR-40/-50/-60/-152, Walid, 300 M-113A2 armored personnel carriers
Artillery: 1,500 85mm, 100mm (including 200 SU-100 self-propelled), 122mm, 130mm, 152mm (including SU-152 self-propelled) and 180mm guns; 122mm, 152mm howitzers; 400 120mm, 160mm and 240mm mortars; about 300 122mm (including Saqr 30), 132mm, 140mm and 240mm multiple rocket launchers; 12 FROG-7, 12 Scud B surface-to-surface missiles
Anti-tank: 900 57mm (including self-propelled), 76mm and 100mm guns; 900 82mm and 107mm recoilless launchers; 1,000 Sagger, Snapper, Swatter, Milan, Beeswing, Swingfire and TOW anti-tank guided weapon
Air defense: 350 ZSU-23-4 and ZSU-57-2 self-propelled anti-aircraft guns; SA-7/-9, 16 Crotale surface-to-air missiles

(On order: 189 M-60A3 main battle tanks; 600 BMR-600, 750 M-113A2 armored personnel carriers; M-109A2 155mm self-propelled howitzers; JPz SK-105 self-propelled anti-tank gun, 52 M-901 self-propelled TOW anti-tank guided weapon armored fighting vehicles; 100 M-106A2 and M-125A2 mortar carriers; 200 TOW launchers, 4,000 missiles [including 2,500 Improved TOW], 2,000 Swingfire anti-tank guided weapons, Skyguard air defense twin 35mm/Sparrow surface-to-air missile systems, 4 Crotale surface-to-air missiles)

Reserves: about 300,000

Navy: 20,000 (15,000 conscripts)

12 submarines: 6 R-class (2 Chinese), 6 Soviet W-class
 5 destroyers: 4 Soviet Skory (1 with 1x2 Styx surface-to-surface missiles), 1 British Z-class
 5 frigates: 2 Spanish F-30 (Descubierta); 3 British (1 Black Swan, 1 Hunt, 1 River [submarine support ship])
24 fast attack craft (missile): 6 Ramadan, with 4 Otomat; 6 October-6 (P-6), with 2 Otomat 8 Soviet Osa-1 with SA-7 surface-to-air missiles, 4 Styx surface-to-surface missiles; 4 Komar,
12 Soviet SO-1 large patrol craft: 6 with BM-21 multiple rocket launchers, some with SA-7 surface-to-air missiles
16 Soviet fast attack craft (torpedo): 2 Shershen, 10 P-6<, 4 P-4<
14 Soviet fast attack craft (gun): 4 Shershen with BM-21 multiple rocket launchers, SA-7 surface-to-air missiles; 10 P-6<
12 Soviet minesweepers: 10 ocean (6 T-43, 4 Yurka), 2 T-301 inshore
 3 SRN-6 hovercraft (may be minelayers)
 3 Soviet Polnocny landing craft, tank
13 Soviet landing craft, utility (9 Vydra, 4 SMBI)
 1 anti-submarine warfare helicopter squadron with 6 Sea King Mark 47
Coastal defense unit (Army manpower, Navy control):
    SSM-4-1 130mm guns, 30 Otomat and Samlet surface-to-surface missiles
(On order: 6 Cormoran fast attack craft [missile], 12 Timsah patrol boats, 14 SRN-6 hovercraft, Otomat surface-to-surface missiles)

Bases: Alexandria, Port Said, Mersa Matruh, Port Tewfiq, Hurghada, Safada

Reserves: 15,000

Air Force: 27,000 (10,000 conscripts); 498 combat ac, 24 combat hel.

1 bomber regiment with 14 Tu-16 (some with AS-5 air-to-surface missiles)
5 fighters, ground attack regiments: 2 with 20 F-16, 44 Chinese F-6; 2 with 50 MiG-17F, 36 Su-7BM; 1 with 53 Mirage 5SDE2
2 reconnaissance squadrons with 6 Mirage 5SDR, 12 MiG-21R/RF, 20 Su-7
1 maritime reconnaissance squadron with 5 Il-28 electronic intelligence air craft: 2 EC-130H
4 helicopter squadrons with 52 Gazelle (24 with HOT anti-tank guided weapons)
1 transport brigade of 5 squadrons with 21 C-130H, 18 Il-14, 10 An-12, 4 Falcon 20 (VIP), 10 DHC-5D Buffalo, 1 Boeing 707, 1 Boeing 737
8 utility helicopter squadrons with 20 Mi-4, 40 Mi-8, 52 SA-342H, 4 SA-342K Gazelle, 25 Commando (2 VIP), 15 CH-47C

Trainers including 15 MiG-15UTI, MiG-21U/US, 10 Alpha Jet, 60 L-29, 60 Gomhouria, 36 Yak-18, Wilga 35/80, 4 Chinese FT-6, 6 Mirage 5SDD, 4F-16B.
Air-to-air missiles: AA-2 Atoll, R-530, Sparrow, Sidewinder
Air-to-surface missiles: AS-1 Kennel, AS-5 Kelt, Maverick, HOT

(Further aircraft in reserve including up to 50 MiG-21, 17 MiG-23BN/U, 72 MiG-17, 67 Su-7, 40 Su-20, 43 F-6, 34 F-4 Phantom, 3 An-24 aircraft; 12 Mi-6 helicopters)

(On order: 100 Chinese F-7 (MiG-21 type), 20 F-16A/B, 20 Mirage 2000, 16 Mirage 5E2 fighters; 35 Alpha Jet [15-A fighters, ground attack, 20-E training]; 4 E-2C airborne early warning; 6 C-130H transport aircraft; 12 Sea King anti-submarine warfare, Super Puma, 24 Cobra with TOW, 15 CH-47, 18 UH-12E, 36 Gazelle [24 with HOT anti-tank guided weapons], 4 AS-61 helicopters; Sparrow, 300 Sidewinder air-to-air missiles; AM-39 Exocet, Maverick air-to-surface missiles)

Reserves: about 20,000

Air Defense Command: 85,000 (50,000 conscripts)

12 centers under construction
 2 air defense divisions; regional brigades
100 missile and anti-aircraft battalions, radar battalions; some 80 SA-2, 65 SA-3 sites; 360 SA-2, 75 SA-6, 6 Improved HAWK, 16 Crotale surface-to-air missiles; 2,500 20mm, 23mm, 37mm, 40mm, 57mm, 85mm and 100mm anti-aircraft guns; Fan Song, Low Blow, Straight Flush missile/gun and Squint Eye, Long Track early warning radars
 3 interceptor brigades: 7 squadrons with 142 MiG-21F/PFS/FL/PFM/M/MF; 2 forming with 40 F-16A, 54 Mirage 5 SDE1

(On order: Chinese CSA-1, Spada, LPD-20 search radar; 6 batteries totalling 72 launchers, 216 Improved HAWK surface-to-air missiles)

Forces Abroad: Iraq, Oman, Sudan (2,000), Somalia, Zaire

Para-Military forces: 139,000: National Guard, 60,000; Frontier Corps, 12,000; Defence and Security, 60,000; Coast Guard, 7,000; 3 Nisr, 6 Crestitalia, 6 Bertram patrol boats, 4 rescue launches.

(On order: 6 31-meter patrol boats)

Source: The Military Balance 1983-1984

Table 6.

TREATIES IN EFFECT EGYPT-USA

Atomic Energy

Description:	Treaty	Date Signed Amendments
Arrangement for the exchange of technical information and cooperation in nuclear saefty matters, with addenda.	TIAS 10170	June 8, 1981
Agreement for cooperation concerning peaceful uses of nuclear energy, with annex.	TIAS 10208	June 29, 1981

Aviation

Agreement concerning the use of Payne Field for international civil air traffic.	3 UST 363 TIAS 2397 151 UNTS 135	June 15, 1945
Air transport agreement.	15 UST 2202 TIAS 5706	May 4, 1964

Canals

Agreement relating to the clearance of mines and unexploded ordnances from the Suez Canal.	25 UST 1474 TIAS 7882	April 25, 1974
Arrangement relating to the salvage and/or removal of sunken vessels and other hazards to navigation from the Suez Canal.	25 UST 1273 TIAS 7859	June 11, 1974
Agreement relating to continued service of a task force to assist Egypt in the clearance of the Suez Canal.	26 UST 2523 TIAS 8170	June 29, 1975

Defense

Agreement extending privileges and immunities to U.S. military personnel in Egypt in connection with joint Egyptian/U.S. Air Force training exercises.	TIAS 9808	June 25, 1980

Source: Treaties in Force, United Nations

Table 7.

TRADE IN MAJOR CONVENTIONAL WEAPONS 1979-84

Supplier	No. ordered	Weapon designation	Weapon description	Year of order	Year of delivery	No. delivered
Austria	100	Cuirassier	LT/TD	1981		
Canada	10	DHC-5D Buffalo	Transport	1981	1982	(6)
China	(60)	F-7	Fighter	1982		
	2	Romeo Class	Submarine	(1980)	1982	2
		SA-2 Guideline	Landmob SAM	1980		
France	2	Agosta Class	Submarine	1978		
	45	Alpha Jet	Adv trainer/strike	1981	1982 (1983)	(5) (15)
		Mirage-2000	Fighter/strike	1982	1983	(5)
	16	Mirage-5SD	Fighter	1981		
		Otomat-2	ShShM	1982		
	(96)	R-440 Crotale	Landmob SAM	1982	1982	(48)
	36	SA-342L Gazelle	Hel	1981		
Italy	(15)	CH-47C Chinook	Hel	1980	1982	(15)
	24	Otomat-1	ShShM	1978	1981	8
	4	S-61R	Hel	1981		
Spain	2	Agosta Class	Submarine	1982		
	600	BMR-600	ICV	1982		
	6	Cormoran Class	FAC	1982		
	2	F-30 Class	Frigate	1982	(1982)	(2)
UK	6	Ramadan Class	FAC	1978	1981	2
		Scorpion FV-101	LT	1982		
	14	SRN-6	Hovercraft	(1980)		
USA	600	AGM-65A	ASM	1980	1980	(75)
	300	AIM-9L	AAM	1982	(1982)	(100)
	2,400	BGM-71A TOW	ATM	1981	1982	2400
	6	C-130H Hercules	Transport	1981	1982	3
	4	E-2C Hawkeye	AEW	1982		
	40	F-16A	Fighter/strike	1980		
	34	F-16A	Fighter/strike	1982		

Source: SIPRI 1983

TRADE IN MAJOR CONVENTIONAL WEAPONS 1979-84

Supplier	No. ordered	Weapon designation	Weapon description	Year of order	Year of delivery	No. delivered
USA	6	F-16B	Fighter/trainer	1982		
	35	F-4 Phantom	Fighter	(1981)		
	79	M-106-A1	APC	1979	1982	(79)
		M-109-A2 155mm	SPH	(1982)		
	400	M-113-A2	APC	1979	1980	(120)
					1981	(120)
					1982	(160)
	570	M-113-A2	APC	1980	1982	(252)
					(1983)	(318)
	41	M-125-A1	APC	1979	1982	41
	34	M-577-A1	CPC	1979	1982	20
					(1983)	(14)
	439	M-60-A3	MBT	1980	1981	128
					1982	183
					(1983)	(120)
					(1984)	(8)
	220	M-60-A3	MBT	1982		
	86	M-88-A1	ARV	1980	1981	16
					1982	13
					(1983)	(57)
	23	M-88-A1	ARV	1982		
	52	M-901 TOW	APC	1980	(1983)	(52)
	36	MIM-23B Hawk	Landmob SAM	1979	1981	18
					1982	(18)
	216	MIM-23B Hawk	Landmob SAM	1981	1982	(108)
	12	Spectre Class	FAC	(1979)		
	(18)	UH-12E	Hel	1982	1982	(18)

Abbreviations:

SAM	= Surface to Air Missile	SPH	= Self-Propelled Howitzer
ShShM	= Ship to Ship Missile	APC	= Armored Personnel Carrier
ICV	= Infantry Combat Vehicle	CPC	= Command Post Carrier
FAC	= Fast Attack Craft	ARV	= Armored Recovery Vehicle
LT	= Light Tank	AEW	= Airborne Early Warning System
ASM	= Air to Surface Missile	MBT	= Main Battle-Gun
ATM	= Anti-Tank Missile	AAM	= Air to Air Missile

Note: Parentheses denote uncertain information

Table 8.

MILITARY EXPENDITURE IN CURRENT AND CONSTANT PRICES
(million LE)

	1975	1976	1977	1978	1979	1981	1982
Current prices	1,631	1,564	1,845	1,000*	1,200*	1,320*	1,450*
Constant prices	4,266	3,709	3,883	1,894*	2,068*	1,886*	1,875*

*years 78-82 imported values only, estimates

Source: SIPRI 1983

Table 9.

MAJOR ARMS SUPPLIERS, CUMULATIVE 1978-1982
(Million current US $)

Soviet Union	30
United States	1,500
France	800
United Kingdom	600
West Germany	260
Italy	290
Romania	20
China	200
Others	480
Total	**4,200**

Source: U.S. Arms Control & Disarmament Agency, 1984

Table 10.
VALUE OF ARMS TRANSFERS

Year	Imports (million US $)		Arms Imports/ Total Imports	Exports (million US $)		Arms Exports/ Total Exports
	Current	Constant		Current	Constant	
1972	550	1,069	61.1	0	0	0.0
1973	850	1,565	92.8	0	0	0.3
1974	230	389	9.7	5	8	0.0
1975	350	543	8.8	0	0	0.0
1976	150	220	3.9	0	0	0.0
1977	250	346	5.1	50	69	2.9
1978	400	516	5.9	90	116	5.2
1979	625	744	16.2	10	11	0.5
1980	550	601	11.3	0	0	0.0
1981	575	575	6.5	30	30	0.9
1982	2,100	1,980	23.1	290	273	9.3

Source: U.S. Arms Control & Disarmament Agency, 1984

Table 11.

MILITARY EXPENDITURE, ARMED FORCES, GNP

	M/E as % of GNP	M/E as % Central Govt. Expend.	per capita (constant 81 prices)	Armed Forces ('000)
1975	30.9	50.5	120	400
1976	22.1	38.3	100	400
1977	21.0	40.4	104	350
1978	13.9	29.6	74	447
1979	11.1	22.6	59	447
1980	10.3	19.7	59	NA
1981	NA	NA	NA	NA
1982	8.2	15.1	50	NA

Source: U.S. Arms Control & Disarmament Agency April, 1984
World Military Expenditures & Arms Transfers 1972-1982

DEMOGRAPHY

Table 12.

POPULATION DENSITY PER SQUARE KILOMETER
(as of October 1981)

Governorate	Density
Cairo	27,092
Alexandria	994
Port Said	4,965
Suez	13
Damietta	1,147
Dakahlia	927
Sharkia	740
Kalyubia	2,019
Kafr El-Sheikh	482
Gharbia	1,374
Menoufia	1,310
Behera	289
Ismailia	300
Giza	2,874
Beni-Suef	994
Fayoum	753
Minya	1,087
Assiut	1,297
Souhag	1,467
Kena	1,090
Aswan	1,067

Source: Demographic Yearbook 1982

Table 13.

POPULATION, RATES OF BIRTH, DEATH, AND NATURAL INCREASE*

	1976	1977	1978	1979	1980	1981	1982
Population (thousands)	37,891	38,794	39,473	40,983	42,289	43,465	44,673
Birth Rates (per thousand)	36.4	37.3	37.2	40.9	40.9	40.2	33.4
Death Rates (per thousand)	11.7	11.8	10.5	11.0	10.9	10.2	9.8
Rate of Natural Increase (%)	2.5	2.6	2.7	3.0	3.0	3.0	2.4
Growth Rate (%)	2.4	2.4	2.4	3.1	3.2	2.8	2.8

* Includes estimates of migrant population

Source: Central Agency for Public Mobilization and Statistics

Table 14.

POPULATION OF MAJOR CITIES (1976) *

Major Cities	Population
Alexandria	2,317,705
Aswan	144,654
Assyut	213,751
Beni-Suef	117,910
Cairo	5,074,016
Dananhur	170,633
El-Mahalla El-Kubra	292,114
Faiyum	166,910
Giza	1,230,446
Ismailia	145,930
Kafr El-Dwar	146,248
Mansura	259,387
Menia	146,366
Port Said	262,760
Shubra El-Khema	394,223
Suez	193,965
Zagazig	202,575

* Date of last official census

Source: Demographic Yearbook 1982

Table 15.

CHIEF DEMOGRAPHIC INDICATORS (1981)

```
Population, total...........................................43,290,000
Population ages % of total
  0-14......................................................39.5
  15-64.....................................................56.9
  65+.......................................................3.54
Population under 20 as % of total...........................50.43
Women ages 15-49 as % of total..............................48.33
Child-woman ratios (per 1,000)..............................654
Urban population as % of total..............................44.3
Crude birth rates...........................................35.7
Crude death rates...........................................11.7
Infant mortality rate (rate per 1,000)......................101.3
Total fertility rates.......................................4.8
Life expectancy, males......................................55.4
Life expectancy, females....................................58.5
```

Source: World Bank 1984

Table 16.

POPULATION BY GOVERNORATE
as of October 13, 1982

Governorate:	Total Population (thousands)	Percent of Total Population
Cairo	5,803	12.90
Alexandria	2,664	5.92
Port Said	358	0.80
Suez	236	0.52
Damietta	676	1.50
Dakahlia	3,218	7.15
Sharkia	3,092	6.87
Kalyubia	2,021	4.49
Kafr El-Sheikh	1,658	3.69
Gharbia	2,669	5.93
Monoufia	2,007	4.46
Behera	2,925	6.50
Ismailia	433	0.96
Giza	2,902	6.45
Beni-Suef	1,314	2.92
Fayoum	1,376	3.06
Minya	2,459	5.46
Assiut	2,015	4.48
Souhag	2,270	5.04
Kena	2,017	4.48
Aswan	724	1.61
Red Sea	66	0.15
El-Wadi El-Gedid	103	0.23
Matrouh	150	0.33
Sinai	165	0.37
Total Population:	**43,321**	**96.27**
Population Abroad:	**1,679**	**3.73**

Source: Official Government Estimates

ECONOMY

Table 17.

ECONOMIC INDICATORS

	1981/82 (million US $)	Annual Growth Rates (%) (constant 1975 Prices)	
National Accounts		1974-80/81	1981/82
GNP at Market Price	25,447	9.8	5.3
Consumption	21,388	6.8	7.6
Gross Investment	7,561	3.0	10.9
Exports of GNFS	7,962	12.5	10.1
Imports of GNFS	11,665	7.1	9.0

Source: World Bank 1983

Table 18.

GROWTH IN GROSS DOMESTIC PRODUCT
(Percent increase)

	1980/81	1981/82	Estimated 1982/83
Gross Domestic Product at Factor Cost	8.7	7.6	6.9
Commodity Sectors	7.3	5.4	5.3
of which: Agriculture	3.5	3.0	2.5
Industry & Mining	8.8	9.0	8.5
Petroleum	18.9	6.1	6.0
Distribution Sectors	10.9	9.9	8.5
Service Sectors	9.2	9.8	8.6

Source: Ministry of Planning and independent estimates

Table 19.

GROSS DOMESTIC PRODUCT AT CURRENT PRICES
(million LE)

	1975	1976	1977	1978	1979	1980/81
Commodity Sectors						
Agriculture	1,468	1,744	2,038	2,286	2,530	3,427
Industry & Mining	880	993	1,120	1,319	1,650	2,144
Petroleum	149	247	468	626	1,908	3,105
Electricity & Public Utilities	88	96	106	121	132	157
Construction	243	279	357	517	647	761
Distribution Sectors						
Transportation, Commun. & Storage	220	260	322	395	586	768
Suez Canal	40	141	169	294	406	543
Trade, Finance & Insurance	772	954	1,188	1,544	2,067	2,498
Service Sectors						
Housing	209	222	244	262	287	321
Other Services	987	1,229	1,522	1,657	1,888	2,454
(Tourism) *	99	127	134	167	190	247
GDP at Factor Cost	5,056	6,165	7,534	9,021	12,101	16,178
Net Indirect Taxes	162	562	810	774	604	768
GDP at Market Prices	5,218	6,727	8,344	9,795	12,705	16,949

* The 1980/81 figure was derived by assuming the same growth rate as for other services.

Source: Ministry of Planning and independent estimates.

Table 20.

GROSS DOMESTIC PRODUCT AT CONSTANT PRICES BY SECTOR
(million LE at 1975 prices)

	1977	1978	1979	1980/81	1981/82
Commodity Sectors					
Agriculture	1,447.2	1,528.0	1,592.0	1,676.0	1,726
Industry & mining	1,012.4	1,068.0	1,152.3	1,307.2	1,425
Petroleum	350.1	427.0	471.0	610.5	648
Construction	263.1	342.0	377.0	407.0	431
Electricity	86.0	103.0	108.0	135.0	128
Distribution Sectors					
Transport, Communication, & storage	288.7	333.0	487.2	562.4	601
Trade & Finance	924.0	1,070.0	1,264.0	1,478.0	1,641
Suez Canal	170.8	201.0	235.1	281.3	309
Service Sectors					
Housing	242.9	259.0	278.0	317.7	350
Public Utilities	21.7	24.0	26.0	30.0	-
Other Services	1,100.0	1,170.0	1,094.0	1,260.0	-
GDP at Factor Cost	5,907.0	6,525.0	7,084.6	8,076.5	8,785.0

Source: Ministry of Planning

BANKING AND FINANCE

Table 21.

FINANCIAL SURVEY

	1979	1980	1981	1982	1983	1984-I
International Liquidity (million US $)						
Foreign Exchange Reserves	529	1,046	688	698	739	852
Gold (mn fine troy ounces)	2.472	2.432	2.432	2.432	2.432	2.432
Gold (national valuation)	104	103	775	578	757	757
Reserve Position in Fund	--	--	28	--	32	--
Commercial Banks (million LE)						
Claims on Government	2,546	3,707	2,812	2,862	3,218	3,535
Claims on Private Sector	2,396	3,480	5,826	6,910	8,902	9,261
Claims on Other Financial Institutions	136	360	589	848	836	821
Foreign Assets	1,922	2,482	2,401	3,011	3,908	3,694
Reserves	803	1,269	2,151	3,226	4,560	4,299
Foreign Liabilities	860	1,441	1,833	1,938	2,634	2,554
Demand Deposits	1,697	1,446	1,780	2,238	2,540	2,463
Time, Saving and Foreign Currency Deposits	2,490	4,158	6,485	9,020	11,385	11,724
Government Deposits	821	1,229	1,547	1,496	1,532	1,541
Capital Accounts Other	752	1,336	2,016	2,397	2,979	3,060
Central Bank (million LE)						
Foreign Assets	763	1,187	1,619	1,667	2,007	2,157
Claims on Government	6,203	6,845	8,810	10,735	13,006	12,938
Claims on Commercial Banks	1,153	1,755	260	216	287	169
Claims on Other Fin. Inst.	121	215	388	659	907	892
Reserves	3,402	4,743	6,596	8,735	11,219	11,110
Foreign Liabilities	3,965	3,880	3,578	3,783	3,314	3,218
Government Deposits	693	1,230	867	846	1,503	1,531
Other	181	148	35	-88	172	296

Source: International Financial Statistics September, 1984

Table 22.

FISCAL SUMMARY
(billion LE)

	1980/81	1981/82	1982/83
Public Revenues			
of which: Taxes	7.4	8.2	9.4
Other	(4.2)	(4.7)	(5.7)
Public Expenditures	10.6	12.9	14.5
of which: Current Expenditures			
& Capital Transfers	(4.6)	(6.0)	(7.7)
Subsidies	(2.2)	(2.2)	(2.0)
Investment	(3.8)	(4.7)	(4.8)
Public Sector Deficit	**3.2**	**4.7**	**5.1**
Source of Financing:			
External	(1.1)	(1.2)	(1.5)
Domestic, Non-Bank	(1.2)	(1.3)	(1.9)
Banking Sector	(0.9)	(2.2)	(1.7)

Source: Ministry of Finance

Table 23.

FACTORS AFFECTING MONETARY EXPANSION
(million LE)

Changes During Period	1978	1979	1980/81	1981/82	Estimate 1982/83
Foreign Assets (net)	-1,526	76	371	-414	147
Domestic Credit	3,026	1,704	2,161	6,088	4,411
Public Sector Claims	2,617	899	496	2,793	2,340
Cent. & Loc. Gov't (net)	(2,463)	(1,598)	(-612)	(2,805)	(2,548)
Public Authorities (net)	(221)	(-442)	(692)	(43)	(-169)
Public Sector Companies	(-66)	(-257)	(416)	(31)	(-39)
Private Sector Claims	140	429	1,212	1,819	863
Claims on other					
Financial Institutions	31	186	300	431	519
Other items (net)	238	190	153	1,045	689
Money & Quasi-money	929	1,097	2,137	3,702	3,353
Money	599	381	914	1,272	1,601
Quasi-money	330	716	1,223	2,430	1,752
Memo item:					
Foreign Currency Deposits	202	174	568	1,510	546
Growth rate (% per year)					
Money & Quasi-money	29	27	34	44	28
Foreign Currency deposits	49	28	50	89	17

Source: Central Bank of Egypt, IMF, and World Bank

Table 24.
SUMMARY OF FISCAL OPERATIONS
(million LE)

	1978	1979	1980/81	1981/82	Estimate 1982/83
Indirect Taxes	1,421.3	1,671.5	2,354.9	2,740.2	3,287.0
Foreign Trade	919.8	905.0	1,329.4	1,573.2	1,651.0
Consumption	360.3	566.8	699.7	812.6	1,217.0
Other Indirect 1/	141.2	199.7	325.8	354.4	419.0
Direct Taxes	725.8	870.1	1,824.0	1,944.7	2,429.0
Personal Income	51.9	55.1	73.2	85.4	110.0
Business Profit	538.4	655.7	1,506.3	1,577.7	1,900.0
Other 2/	135.5	159.3	244.5	281.6	419.0
Total Tax Revenue	2,147.1	2,541.6	4,178.9	4,684.9	5,716.0
Non-tax Gov't Revenue 3/	147.2	267.2	494.0	587.0	623.0
Total Revenue	2,294.0	2,808.8	4,672.9	5,271.9	6,339.0
Public Economic Sector Surplus	1,012.3	875.0	2,699.9	2,958.7	3,052.0
Transferred Profits	539.3	501.0	1,735.5	1,714.7	1,852.0
Investment Self-financing	473.0	374.0	964.4	1,244.0	1,200.0
Total Public Revenue	3,306.3	3,683.8	7,372.8	8,230.6	9,391.0
Service Agencies Expenditures	2,037.0	2,494.7	3,691.0	4,893.5	9,391.0
Public Authority Deficit	58.0	60.0	67.3	100.4	128.0
Subsidies	710.0	1,352.0	2,166.4	2,192.1	2,000.0
Net Capital Expenditure 4/	443.0	643.0	864.9	1,030.0	1,100.0
Investment Expenditure	2,311.0	2,547.0	3,765.6	4,761.0	4,800.0
Total Public Expenditure	5,559.0	7,096.0	10,555.2	12,887.1	14,494.0

Source: Ministry of Finance

SUMMARY OF FISCAL OPERATIONS
(million LE)

	1978	1979	1980/81	1981/82	Estimate 1982/83
Gross Public Sector Deficit	2,252.7	3,412.9	3,182.4	4,656.5	5,103.0
External Financing of Deficits 5/	882.0	1,135.3	1,101.9	1,212.4	1,538.0
Domestic Financing of Deficit	1,370.7	2,277.6	2,080.5	3,444.1	3,565.0
Non-bank Domestic Financing	543.7	695.0	1,206.4	1,261.4	1,876.0
Bank Financing	827.0	1,582.6	874.1	2,182.7	1,689.0
Memo Items					
Total Expenditure as % of GDP	57	56	61	63	60
Total Revenue as % of GDP	34	29	43	40	39
Total Deficit as % of GDP	23	27	18	23	21

1/ Includes: Stamp taxes and miscellaneaous other taxes.
2/ Includes: Taxes on property, estate duties, taxes on immovable property and local government tax revenue.
3/ Includes: Fees, miscellaneous non-tax revenue and local government non-tax revenue.
4/ Includes: Government debt installments on domestic and foreign debt, net capital transfer to public economic authorities and public sector companies and miscellaneous capital expenditure by the government.
5/ Gross foreign financing of the budget.

Table 25.

CONSUMER PRICE INDEX FOR URBAN POPULATION

	1979	1980/81	1981/82	1982/83
Foodstuffs (52.5) *	277.3	393.8	458.8	562.9
Cereals (11.2)	134.4	191.3	216.0	235.7
Pulses (6.6)	305.4	512.2	512.7	602.9
Meat, Fish and Eggs (13.1)	383.7	504.2	572.7	762.3
Dairy (5.9)	336.9	462.5	545.6	660.2
Vegetables (3.8)	336.8	424.7	493.6	586.4
Fruits (2.9)	392.4	422.7	644.5	1,004.1
Housing (15.7)	111.2	114.3	113.7	118.5
Furniture and Other Durables (1.3)	187.7	201.3	283.9	298.4
Clothing (8.4)	247.5	310.6	344.8	386.2
Transportation and Communication (4.4)	185.6	207.9	313.2	313.2
Services (9.9)	244.2	277.5	329.5	380.6
Personal Expenses (7.8)	187.9	213.7	223.0	231.3
All Items (100)	**233.5**	**307.0**	**356.0**	**425.8**

* The numbers in parentheses are indicative commodity weights based on the commodity weights employed in five regional subindices and population weights for these regions.

Source: Central Agency for Public Mobilization and Statistics

Table 26.

DISTRIBUTION OF PRIVATE SECTOR CREDIT
(million LE)

Change During Period	1979	1980	1980/81	1981
Agriculture	6.5	6.4	37.7	76.5
Industry	109.0	191.5	284.4	390.8
Trade	200.6	272.8	481.3	897.2
Services	48.2	147.4	232.9	344.8
Household	36.8	99.9	152.8	96.9
Total	**401.1**	**718.0**	**1,189.2**	**1,806.2**

Source: Central Bank of Egypt

Table 27.

INTEREST RATE SURVEY
(in percent)

	\multicolumn{7}{c}{Effective From}						
	Mar 1 1977	June 1 1978	Jan 1 1979	Apr 1 1980	June 1 1980	Jan 1 1981	Aug 1 1981
Commercial Banks							
Time and Savings Deposit Rate							
7 days	-	-	4	4.5	4.5	5	5
15 days	2.5	4	5	5.5	5.5	6	6
1 month	3.0	4.5	5.5	6	6.5	7.5	7.5
3 months	4	5.5	6	7	7.5	8.5	8.5
6 months	4.5	6	6.5	7.5	8	9	9.5
1 year	5	6.5	7	8	9	9.5	10
2 years	5	7	7.5	8.5	9.5	10.5	10.5
3 years	5	7	8	9	10	11	11
5 years	5	7	8.5	9.5	10.5	11.5	11.5
Savings	5	5	6	7	8	8.5	8.5
Lending Rates							
Min. rate	8	9	10	11	12	13	13
Max. rate	9	11	12	13	14	15	15
Central Bank							
Discount Rate	7	8	9	10	11	12	12

Source: Central Bank of Egypt

Table 28.

LENDING RATES OF INTEREST

		1980		1981		1982
		1/4	1/6	1/1	1/8	1/7
Industrial & Agricultural Sector	Min.	11	12	13	13	-
	Max.	13	14	15	15	15
Service Sector	Min.	11	12	13	13	13
	Max.	13	14	15	15	15
Trade Sector	Min.	11	12	13	13	16
	Max.	13	14	15	15	-

Source: Central Bank of Egypt

Table 29.

EXCHANGE RATES
(US Dollars per LE: end of period)

Year	Rate
1978	2.5556
1979	1.4286
1980	1.4286
1981	1.4286
1982	1.4286
1983	1.4286
1984 July	1.4286

Source: International Financial Statistics September 1984

BUDGET AND PLANNING

Table 30.
BUDGET OUTLINE
(million LE)

Current Budget	1981/82	1982/83	1983/84
Revenue:			
Sovereignty			
Company taxes (profits)	2,039	1,812	--
Customs duties	1,459	1,951	--
Consumption taxes	875	1,217	--
All other	1,107	944	--
Sub total	5,480	5,924	6,916
Current resources			
Petroleum authority surplus	1,215	1,195	--
Suez Canal authority surplus	358	312	--
Other	832	1,262	--
Sub total	2,410	2,769	3,070
Total Current Revenue	**7,890**	**8,693**	**9,986**
Expenditure:			
Wages	2,100	2,444	2,935
Subsidies	2,000	2,040	1,686
Armed forces	1,287	1,742	
Debt interest	601	952	5,282
Other current	1,160	1,576	
Total Expenditure	**7,148**	**8,754**	**9,903**
Current surplus (deficit)	742	(61)	83
Capital transfers budget:			
Expenditure less			
internal funding	1,156	1,683	1,501
Investment budget:			
Expenditure less			
internal funding	3,112	3,101	3,594
Total deficit	**3,526**	**4,845**	**5,012**

Source: Ministry of Finance

Table 31.

FUNCTIONAL CLASSIFICATION OF CURRENT EXPENDITURE
(million LE)

	1977	1978	1979	1980/81	1981/82
Gen Public Services 1/	502	492	895	1,709	2,114
Defense 2/	599	709	772	1,034	1,366
Education	244	279	365	359	608
Health	80	96	114	140	213
Community & Social Services	30	54	86	106	109
Economic Services	69	90	101	134	199
Agriculture	62	84	48	61	99
Irrigation	-	-	50	53	73
Transportation and Communication	7	6	3	20	28
Central Govt Current Expenditure	1,701	2,037	2,495	3,691	4,894
Local Govt Current Expenditure	117	135	162	209	285

1/ Includes Investment Fund current operating expenditure, Treasury Fund outlay for pensions and contingencies, and services agencies expenditure.

2/ Includes emergency fund deficit.

Source: Ministry of Finance

Table 32.

**TOTAL INVESTMENT OF THE FIVE-YEAR
PLAN BY PUBLIC/PRIVATE SECTOR**
(million LE, 1981/82 prices)

	Public Sector		Private Sector	
	Value	%	Value	%
Agriculture	2,720.7	10.2	1,019.0	12.5
Industry & Mining	6,841.9	25.7	1,775.0	21.7
Petroleum	1,336.7	5.0	--	--
Electricity	2,844.8	10.7	59.1	0.7
Construction	526.7	2.0	415.0	5.1
Public Utilities	2,858.1	10.7	--	--
Total Commodity Sectors	17,128.9	64.3	3,268.1	40.1
Transport, Storage & Communication	5,533.9	20.7	245.2	3.0
Suez Canal	335.0	1.3	--	--
Trade and Finance	500.3	1.9	80.0	1.0
Total Productive Services Sector	6,369.2	23.9	325.2	4.0
Housing	264.0	1.0	4,372.8	53.6
Others	2,863.9	10.8	198.5	2.4
Total Social Services Sectors	3,127.4	11.8	4,571.3	56.0
Total Fixed Investment	26,626.0	100.0	8,164.6	100.0
Investment Expenditure	585.5	--	107.0	--
Grand Total	2,7214.5	--	8,271.6	--

Source: Ministry of Planning Estimates

Table 33.

TOTAL INVESTMENT OF THE FIVE-YEAR PLAN DISTRIBUTED BY SECTOR
(million LE, 1981/82 prices)

	Plan Total Value	%	Actual Share (1977-1981/84)
Agriculture	3,739.7	10.7	8.4
Industry & Mining	8,616.9	24.8	29.2
Petroleum	1,336.7	3.8	2.8
Electricity	2,903.9	8.4	6.3
Construction	941.7	2.7	3.6
Public Utilities	2,858.1	8.2	6.0
Total Commodity Sectors	20,397.0	58.6	56.3
Transport, Storage & Communication	5,779.1	16.6	17.9
Suez Canal	335.0	1.0	6.0
Trade and Finance	580.3	1.6	2.7
Total Productive Services Sector	6,694.4	19.2	6.6
Housing	4,636.8	13.3	8.9
Others	3,062.4	8.9	8.2
Total Social Services Sectors	7,699.2	22.2	12.1
Total Fixed Investment	34,790.6	100.0	100.0

Memo Items:

Foreign Currency Component
 as % of Total Plan Plan Investment)   36.0%
Local Currency Component   64.0%

Source: Ministry of Planning Estimates, 1983

Table 34.

BUDGET HISTORY
(million LE)

	1976	1977	1978	1979	1980
Revenue					
Current Revenue	4,777.8	5,402.0	6,516.0	8,521.6	4,641.8
Sovereignty Revenue	1,341.1	1,780.2	2,115.9	--	3,171.8
Current & Transfer Rev.	3,436.7	3,621.8	4,400.2	--	1,470.0
Capital Revenue	1,196.5	1,648.6	2,366.9	1,714.0	454.3
Sundry	887.8	1,027.4	1,246.3	187.5	134.0
Loans & Credit	308.7	621.2	1,120.6	1,526.5	32.3
Total Revenue	5,974.3	7,050.6	8,883.0	10,235.6	5,096.1
Expenditure					
Current Expenditure	4,777.8	5,402.0	6,516.1	9,175.0	4,918.5
Wages	768.2	937.7	1,100.0	1,257.8	1,343.9
Current & Transfer Exp.	4,009.6	4,464.3	5,416.1	7,917.2	3,574.6
Capital Expenditure	1,196.5	1,648.6	2,336.9	3,749.5	942
Investment	501.7	765.9	1,321.9	1,684.9	--
Capital Transfers	694.8	882.7	1,045.0	2,064.6	942
Total Expenditure	5,974.3	7,050.6	8,883.0	12,924.5	5,860.5

Source: People's Assembly - Plan and Budgetary Committee Report

Table 35.

PROPOSED INDUSTRIAL INVESTMENT
(1982-1987)

	mn LE	% of Total
Food Industries	1,417	23.4
Textiles	1,154	19.1
Mining	914	15.1
Chemicals	750	12.4
Industrial Complexes	655	10.8
Metal Works	523	8.6
Electronics	300	5.0
Sinai	83	1.4
Total (inc. others)	**6,057**	**100.0**

Source: Ministry of Industry and Mining Resources

DEBT

Table 36.

DEBT SERVICE DUE ON MEDIUM AND LONG-TERM DEBT
(outstanding as of June 30, 1982 *)
(million US $)

Debt Category	1982/83	1983/84	1984/85	1985/86
Suppliers Credits				
Amortization	816.3	617.7	498.5	379.4
Interest	--	--	--	--
Financial Markets				
Amortization	228.0	227.8	198.4	393.8
Interest	173.8	149.0	124.8	112.4
Multilateral Institutions				
Amortization	292.6	346.9	390.3	428.6
Interest	152.2	152.0	149.8	141.3
World Bank Group				
Amortization	32.7	43.3	68.9	91.0
Interest	63.9	77.0	88.4	93.9
Arab Fund (incl. GODE)				
Amortization	251.4	278.5	276.6	278.4
Interest	82.1	66.7	51.3	35.7
Other				
Amortization	8.5	25.1	44.8	59.2
Interest	6.2	8.3	10.1	11.7
Bilateral Lenders				
Amortization	457.1	512.3	572.6	423.7
Interest	246.5	268.8	272.4	266.3
of which:				
DAC				
Amortization	100.1	122.3	194.3	274.1
Interest	144.6	166.7	185.0	191.3
OPEC				
Amortization	288.6	287.3	275.5	77.5
Interest	91.3	78.9	66.3	56.8
CPE				
Amortization	68.4	102.7	102.8	72.2
Interest	10.6	23.2	21.1	18.2
Total Debt Service				
Amortization	1,794.0	1,704.6	1,659.8	1,625.6
Interest	572.5	569.8	547.0	520.0

Source: Ministry of Finance, Central Bank of Egypt, and independent estimates.

DEBT SERVICE DUE ON MEDIUM AND LONG TERM DEBT

(million US $)

Debt Category	1986/87	1987/88	1988/89	1989/90
Suppliers Credits				
Amortization	320.3	279.8	145.6	17.2
Interest	--	--	--	--
Financial Markets				
Amortization	94.0	79.0	72.0	58.0
Interest	51.9	36.9	31.7	10.0
Multilateral Institutions				
Amortization	438.1	438.6	156.2	135.9
Interest	126.8	108.5	97.1	91.1
World Bank Group				
Amortization	98.4	100.4	104.6	105.4
Interest	94.1	90.6	85.0	78.9
Arab Fund (incl. GODE)				
Amortization	282.5	285.6	15.9	8.5
Interest	21.1	7.0	4.7	2.5
Other				
Amortization	57.2	52.6	35.7	22.0
Interest	11.6	10.9	7.4	9.7
Bilateral Lenders				
Amortization	435.5	455.8	466.1	458.6
Interest	258.2	249.5	235.4	221.3
of which:				
DAC				
Amortization	295.8	321.5	338.4	352.5
Interest	188.5	184.8	175.6	165.7
OPEC				
Amortization	77.7	76.6	71.7	50.2
Interest	54.1	51.4	48.8	46.7
CPE				
Amortization	62.0	57.7	56.0	55.9
Interest	15.6	13.3	11.0	8.9
Total Debt Service				
Amortization	1,287.9	1,253.2	839.9	669.7
Interest	436.9	394.9	364.2	322.4

* Does not include rescheduling and repayment of arrears.

Table 37.

STRUCTURE OF OUTSTANDING EXTERNAL OBLIGATIONS
(million US $)

	1977 $	1977 %	1978 $	1978 %	1979 $	1979 %
Suppliers Credit	627.3	8	661.7	7	1,093.4	10
Financial Markets	650.6	8	751.0	8	763.6	7
Multilateral Loans	1,564.9	19	2,331.0	23	2,634.0	22
of which IBRD	86.6	1	143.1	1	258.4	2
IDA	167.9	2	212.5	2	267.4	2
GODE	1,225.0	15	1,725.0	17	1,725.0	15
Bilateral Loans	5,249.6	65	6,176.1	62	6,919.9	61
DAC	1,627.3	20	2,497.4	25	3,290.7	29
OPEC	2,930.7	36	3,011.7	30	3,026.2	27
CPE	691.6	9	667.0	7	603.0	5
Total MLT Public Debt	8,092.4	100	9,919.8	100	11,410.9	100
Memo Items:						
MLT Private Debt	18		75		185	
Total MLT	8,110.4		9,994.8		11,595.9	
Stock of Short-Term Debt	555.7		443.4		721.7	
Total Debt	8,666.1		10,438.2		12,317.6	

Source: Ministry of Finance and Central Bank of Egypt

STRUCTURE OF OUTSTANDING EXTERNAL OBLIGATIONS
(million US $)

	1980/81 $	1980/81 %	1981/82 $	1981/82 %
Suppliers Credit	1,945.6	14	2,270.3	15
Financial Markets	779.9	6	753.4	5
Multilateral Loans	2,973.2	22	3,155.2	21
of which IBRD	484.9	4	576.6	4
IDA	357.7	3	447.2	3
GODE	1,725.0	13	1,725.0	13
Bilateral Loans	7,954.4	58	8,776.9	59
DAC	4,540.6	33	5,350.2	36
OPEC	2,817.2	21	2,809.0	19
CPE	596.6	4	617.7	4
Total MLT Public Debt	13,653.1	100	14,955.8	100
Memo Items:				
MLT Private Debt	320		455	
Total MLT	13,973.1		15,410.8	
Stock of Short-Term Debt	974.2		1,169.7	
Total Debt	**14,947.3**		**16,580.5**	

Table 38.

CIVILIAN PUBLIC EXTERNAL DEBT SERVICE 1980-1984
(million US $)

	1980	1981	1982	1983	1984
International Organizations	268.4	344.9	529.6	500.0	520.2
Amortization	123.2	190.3	368.2	343.3	372.2
of which: repurchases of IMF credit	(72.9)	(131.1)	(41.7)	(2.7)	(--)
Interest	145.2	154.6	161.4	156.6	148.0
of which: IMF charges	(16.3)	(8.7)	(2.4)	(1.8)	(1.7)
Foreign Governments	559.0	800.3	687.6	692.6	696.2
Amortization	303.5	532.2	416.7	424.0	433.1
Interest	255.5	268.1	270.9	268.6	263.1
Financial Institutions	215.2	260.1	289.6	272.2	219.9
Amortization	110.5	152.0	193.6	195.9	161.4
Interest	104.7	108.1	96.0	76.3	58.5
Supplier's Credits	782.1	680.1	336.5	130.0	125.0
Amortization	781.4	680.1	336.5	130.0	125.0
Interest	0.7	--	--	--	--
Total	**1,824.6**	**2,085.8**	**1,843.3**	**1,594.7**	**1,561.4**
Amortization	1,318.5	1,554.5	1,315.1	1,093.3	1,081.7
Interest	506.1	531.3	528.2	501.4	469.7

Source: IBRD

ENERGY

Table 39.
PRODUCTION AND DISTRIBUTION OF PETROLEUM, NATRUAL GAS & PETROLEUM PRODUCTS
(million metric tons)

	1975	1979	1980/81	1981/82	1982/83
Total Output of Crude Petroleum	11.7	26.3	31.0	32.5	34.4
Foreign Companies' Share	2.9	5.6	5.4	6.0	6.8
Egyptian Share	8.8	20.7	25.6	26.5	27.6
Used for Refining 1/	10.0	12.5	15.1	14.9	16.9
Net Exports	2.4	8.4	10.5	11.6	10.7
Domestic Consumption of Refined Products 2/	7.4	9.9	11.7	12.7	15.1
Production 3/	8.6	11.4	13.4	14.5	16.4
Net Exports	1.2	1.5	1.7	1.8	1.3
Natural Gas Output	NA	0.9	1.8	1.9	2.2

1/ Difference reflects refining losses and changes in stocks.
2/ Derived residually and includes changes in stocks.
3/ Preliminary estimates.

Source: Egyptian General Petroleum Corporation

Table 40.
PRODUCTION OF PETROLEUM PRODUCTS
(thousand metric tons)

Product:	1978	1979	Jan.-June 1980	80/81	July-Dec. 1981	Official Projections 81/82	82/83
Butane	74	141	78	224	122	196	364
Gasoline/Naptha	1,711	1,771	1,001	1,989	1,018	2,225	2,403
Kerosene	1,464	1,454	829	1,489	757	1,750	1,984
Jet Fuel	178	181	77	154	86	270	340
Gas Oil & Diesel Fuel	2,182	2,312	1,227	2,621	1,345	2,620	2,958
Fuel Oil	5,466	5,527	3,222	6,767	3,757	7,286	8,386
Asphalt	192	202	126	292	142	235	270
Natural Gas	74	141	78	224	122	196	364

Source: Egyptian General Petroleum Corporation

Table 41.

PETROLEUM PRODUCTION
(million metric tons)

	1977	1978	1979	1980/81	1981/82	Estimate 1982/83
By Location:	20.9	24.4	26.3	31.0	32.2	34.4
El Morgan, July and Ramadan	14.4	17.4	18.6	22.6	23.4	25.2
Other Red Sea & Western Desert	1.5	1.4	1.5	1.0	1.0	1.0
Sinai	3.7	4.4	5.1	5.9	6.5	6.9
By Share:						
Cost Recovery Exports	3.1	4.3	5.1	6.2	6.6	7.0
To Cover Actual Costs	1.6	2.7	2.5	1.8	2.3	2.9
Returned to EGPC	1.5	1.6	2.6	4.4	4.2	4.1
Profit Oil	16.5	18.9	20.2	23.8	24.9	26.2
Egyptian Share	14.8	16.2	17.0	20.2	21.0	22.3
Partner's Share	1.7	2.7	3.2	3.6	3.7	3.9
GPC Production	1.3	1.2	1.1	1.1	1.1	1.1
Total Egyptian Share	17.1	18.8	20.7	25.6	26.5	27.6
(plus purchases of crude oil)	0.5	0.2	0.2	--	--	--
Used for Refining	11.1	11.9	12.3	14.3	15.5	17.2
Change in Stocks	0.5	0.2	0.2	0.8	-0.6	-0.3
Exports	6.0	7.9	8.4	10.5	11.6	10.7
Partner's Share	3.8	5.6	5.6	5.4	6.0	6.8
Exports	3.3	5.4	5.4	5.4	5.4	--
Sales to Egypt	0.5	0.2	0.2	--	0.6	--

Source: Egyptian General Petroleum Corporation

Table 42.

EGYPTIAN OIL AND GAS DISCOVERIES 1982

Company/ Discovery Well	Depth	Thickness of Pay Zone	Formation/ Geological Age	Output
Gulf of Suez				
Gupco				
GS 306-1	2,395-2,405 m	9.14 m	Karim	1,759 b/d
GS 345-2	2,274-2,278 m	4.27 m	Karim	3,457 b/d
	2,282-2,288 m	6.10 m	Karim	3,770 b/d
GS 346-1	2,207-2,216 m	9.14 m	Karim	2,889 b/d
GS 356-1	2,083-2,090 m	6.71 m	Karim	3,349 b/d
	2,124-2,133 m	9.45 m	Karim	3,935 b/d
S Ghara 404-1	2,841-2,862 m	21.33 m	Nakhl	1,890 b/d
	2,981-2,987 m	6.10 m	Nubian Sands	4,000 b/d
	3,054-3,060 m	6.10 m	Nubian Sands	4,600 b/d
Total				
S Ramadan 1A	3,350-3,546 m	16 m	Eocene	600 b/d
	3,590-3,633 m	43 m	Upper Senonian	3,500 b/d
	3,673-3,719 m	46 m	Lower Senonian	1,600 b/d
Esso				
E Zeit 391-A	2,546-2,565 m	19.20 m	Rudeis	3,169 b/d
	3,330-3,335 m	5.18 m	Nakhl	2,755 b/d
	3,520-3,566 m	45.72 m	Lower Senonian	304 b/d
Eastern Desert (West of Suez Gulf)				
Canadian Superior				
E Esh el-Mellaha 1	1,116-1,122 m	6.10 m	Lower Miocene	898 b/d
GPC				
NE Bihar 1	1,827-1,832 m	5 m	Karim	377 b/d

Source: Egyptian General Petroleum Corporation

EGYPTIAN OIL AND GAS DISCOVERIES 1982

Company/ Discovery Well	Depth	Thickness of Pay Zone	Formation/ Geological Age	Output
Mediterranean Offshore (Off Northwest Sinai)				
IEOC Port Fuad Marine 1				

	3,012-3,918 m	6 m	Upper Miocene
			  gas
			  condensates
				448,000 m^3/d
				648 b/d

	3,027-3,043 m	16 m	Upper Miocene
			  gas
			  condensates
				467,000 m^3/d
				674 b/d

Western Desert				
Shell Sitra 1-1	2,950-2,963 m	13 m	Bahariya	750 b/d
Badr al-Din 2-1				

	2,273-2,278 m	5 m	Abu Ruwash C
			  gas
			  condensates
				280,368 m^3/d
				288 b/d

	2,395-2,400 m	5 m	Bahariya	220,896 m^3/d 250 b/d

	2,441-2,455 m	14 m	Bahariya
			  gas
			  condensates
				164,256 m^3/d
				168 b/d

GPC
  Y-2
	2,270-2,300 m	30 m	Bahariya
			  gas
			  condensates
				555,072 m^3/d
				889 b/d

Table 43.

REFINERY LOCATION, OWNERSHIP AND CAPACITY

Site	Company	Capacity(b/d)
Alexandria (Ameriyeh)	El-Nasr Petroleum	50,000
Suez	El-Nasr Petroleum	17,000
Suez	Suez Petroleum Processing	18,000
Tanta	Suez Petroleum Processing	16,000
Musturid	Suez Petroleum Processing	74,000
Alexandria	Alexandria Petroleum Co.	60,000
Total		**235,000**

Source: EIU Quarterly Economic Review, Annual Supplement 1984

Table 44.

ENERGY SUPPLY AND DEMAND, 1978-1982
(thousand tons, unless otherwise noted)

Production	1978	1979	1980	1981	1982
Crude Oil	24,417	25,078	28,029	32,500	33,361
Oil Products	11,060	11,387	13,085	13,210	13,500*
Natural Gas (mn cu m)	1,039	1,571	2,267	2,432	2,700*
Electricity (mn kwh)	15,150	16,750	18,520	18,590	19,000*
Imports					
Oil Products	254	115	29	600	
Coal ('000)	755	314	702	1,107	1,000*
Exports					
Crude Oil	4,270	5,246	8,007	10,000	10,200*
Oil Products	1,313	1,452	1,536	1,505	2,000*
Consumption					
Oil	10,001	10,140	11,797	11,808	12,000*

* Estimated to provide a consistent series

Source: UN Yearbook of World Energy Statistics, 1982

Table 45.

PETROLEUM PRODUCTS: PRODUCTION, CONSUMPTION, EXPORTS
(thousand metric tons) *

	1979	1980/81	1981/82	1982/83
Gasoline & Naphtha				
Production	1,771	1,989	2,091	2,305
Consumption	1,085	1,277	1,363	1,664
Net Exports	686	712	728	641
Kerosene				
Production	1,454	1,489	1,571	1,966
Consumption	1,454	1,489	1,706	1,966
Net Export	--	--	-135	--
Jet fuel				
Production	181	154	167	169
Consumption	256	420	463	347
Net Exports	-75	-266	-296	-178
Gas Oil & Diesel Fuel				
Production	2,312	2,621	2,634	2,827
Consumption	2,151	2,817	3,218	3,678
Net Exports	161	-196	-584	-851
Fuel Oil				
Production	5,527	6,767	7,744	8,699
Consumption	4,825	5,533	5,968	7,014
Net Exports	702	1,234	1,776	1,685
Asphalt				
Production	202	292	304	474
Consumption	202	292	304	474
Net Exports	--	--	--	--
Natural Gas				
Production	863	1,810	1,924	2,192
Consumption	863	1,810	1,924	2,192
Net Exports	--	--	--	--
Butane Gas				
Production	141	242	243	269
Consumption	357	392	450	492
Net Exports	-216	-168	-207	-223
Total				
Production	12,451	15,346	16,678	18,901
Consumption	11,193	14,030	15,396	17,827
Net Exports	1,258	1,316	1,282	1,027

* Consumption is derived as a residual and includes stock adjustments.

Source: Egyptian General Petroleum Corporation

Table 46.

CRUDE PETROLEUM EXPORTS BY SOURCE
(thousand metric tons)

Type:	1977	1978	1979	Jan-June 1980	July-July 80/81	July-Dec. 1981	Official proj. 81/82
Suez Blend	839	2,338	2,213	1,287	3,404	1,811	3,359
Belayim Blend	2,290	1,806	2,439	1,127	2,491	1,778	3,648
Mixed Gharib and EPEDCO	1,333	1,338	1,124	558	1,252	658	976
Cost Recovery	1,526	1,629	2,609	1,938	3,381	1,729	3,521
Western Desert	--	--	--	--	--	--	--
Total	5,988	7,111	8,385	4,910	10,528	5,976	11,504

Source: Egyptian General Petroleum Corporation

Table 47.

EXPORTS AND IMPORTS OF CRUDE PETROLEUM PRODUCTS
(volume in mn bbl; value in mn US $)

	1977	1978	1979	1980/81	1981/82	Estimate 1982/83
Exports						
Crude Oil *						
Volume	43.3	50.0	60.6	75.6	83.5	77.1
Value	404.2	482.2	657.1	1,470.0	2,559.7	2,182.4
Petroleum Products						
Volume	14.1	16.1	12.6	17.3	23.0	20.5
Value	213.3	258.1	408.4	619.6	728.8	628.3
Imports						
Petroleum Products						
Volume	0.8	2.0	2.1	7.9	11.5	10.9
Value	14.7	41.1	85.3	295.4	432.2	402.9

* Includes cost recovery

Source: Egyptian General Petroleum Corporation

Table 48.

PETROLEUM EXPORT PRICE
(US $/barrel)

Effective Date/ Period Averages	Morgan Blend	Belayim Blend	Ras Gharib Blend	Weighted Avg Price
1978				
From Oct. 1	12.81	11.57	10.73	11.89
1979				
From Jan. 1	13.45	12.23	11.40	12.54
From Mar. 1	16.50	15.05	14.06	15.41
From April 1	17.15	15.32	14.33	15.83
From June 1	20.50	17.60	16.90	18.57
From July 1	32.50	26.50	21.50	27.83
From Oct. 1	32.50	27.50	21.50	28.25
From Dec. 1	34.00	28.50	22.50	29.44
1980				
From Jan. 1	34.18	29.15	23.68	30.30
From Mar. 1	34.13	29.24	24.00	30.37
From July 1	34.03	29.22	24.00	30.60
From Dec. 1	36.00	31.00	26.00	32.51
1981				
From Jan. 1	40.50	37.00	32.00	37.79
From April 1	37.50	35.50	31.50	35.75
From May 1	36.00	33.00	30.00	33.90
From June 1	33.00	30.00	27.00	30.90
From July 1	33.00	30.00	27.00	30.84
From Nov. 1	34.00	31.00	29.00	32.28
1982				
From Jan. 1	34.00	31.00	28.00	32.12
From Feb. 1	33.00	29.00	26.70	30.64
1979	24.56	20.90	17.70	21.68
1980	34.26	29.36	24.09	30.85
1979/80	33.45	28.18	22.75	29.29
1980/81	36.18	32.22	27.54	33.29
July-Dec. 1980	34.36	29.52	24.33	30.92
July-Dec. 1981	33.33	30.33	27.67	31.32

Source: Egyptian General Petroleum Corporation

INDUSTRY

Table 49.
INDUSTRIAL PRODUCTION
(thousand metric tons, unless otherwise stated)

	1977	1978	1979	1980/81	1981/82
Spinning and Weaving					
Cotton yarn	210	212	218	239	245
Cotton textiles (mn sq m)	905	918	950	980	1,005
Foodstuffs					
Sugar	614	629	632	619	599
Cheese	149	161	160	183	187
Preserved fruits and vegetables	41	40	51	60	60
Cottonseed oil	116	169	168	202	202
Oilseed cakes	430	431	433	540	548
Soft drinks (mn bottles)	984	1,389	1,424	2,222	2,003
Beer (mn liters)	39	42	36	46	51
Cigarettes (billion)	25	27	30	33	36
Chemicals					
Sulfuric acid	27	30	31	21	21
Superphosphates	513	502	483	474	512
Ammonium nitrate*	622	698	851	3,345	4,121
Tires (thousands)	903	857	933	1,106	1,218
Engineering Products					
Cars (units)	12,817	14,562	15,670	18,734	17,035
Trucks and tractors (units)	4,445	4,101	5,087	4,899	6,429
Buses (units)	475	465	552	622	705
Refrigerators (thousands)	129	138	190	259	424
Televisions (thousands)	138	166	228	406	557
Metallurgical Products					
Reinforcing bars	230	249	302	281	275
Steel sections	128	157	177	179	209
Steel sheets	235	229	264	380	313
Cast iron	78	109	112	24	61
Aluminum	90	101	102	134	140
Mining Products					
Phosphate	468	483	527	523	499

* At 31.0 percent nitrogen equivalent

Source: Ministry of Industry

Table 50.

SUBSIDIES PAID BY CENTRAL GOVERNMENT
(million LE)

	1979	1980	Prelim. Actuals 1980/81	Budget est. 1981/82
General Authority for Supply Commodities	879.8	472.0	1,703.0	1,473.1
Cairo and Alexandria Public Transport Authorities	27.4	12.2	26.3	31.7
Agricultural Credit Corporation	0.1	0.1	5.3	4.0
Agricultural Stabilization Fund	101.9	50.4	119.3	132.8
Textile Corporation	50.6	26.5	98.0	69.9
Petroleum Corporation	40.0	29.8	80.0	91.6
Cooperative Building Authority	2.3	3.0	6.9	16.2
Government Credit Banks	19.7	9.1	31.2	40.3
Press Paper Subsidies	3.8	--	6.7	--
Industrial Output Subsidies	41.3	5.0	58.3	52.0
Price Adjustment Fund	--	--	--	--
Other	63.0	31.9	59.5	88.4
Total	**1,229.9**	**640.0**	**2,194.5**	**2,000.0**

Source: Ministry of Finance

AGRICULTURE

Table 51.
PRODUCTION OF MAJOR AGRICULTURAL CROPS
(production in thousand metric tons; area planted in thousands of feddans; yield in metric tons/feddan) 1/

Agricultural Year Ended October 31	1978/79	1979/80	1980/81	1981/82
Winter Crops				
Wheat				
Production	1,856	1,796	1,938	2,017
Area planted	1,391	1,326	1,400	1,374
Yield	1.33	1.35	1.39	1.47
Horsebeans 2/				
Production	236	213	208	260
Area planted	250	245	238	274
Yield	0.95	0.87	0.87	0.95
Onions 3/				
Production	157	311	328	296
Area planted	23	39	39	36
Yield	6.77	8.49	8.33	8.13
Berseem (clover)				
Area planted	2,783	2,711	2,778	2,705
Summer & Autumn Crops				
Cotton				
Production (lint)	484	529	539	461
Area planted	1,195	1,245	1,178	1,066
Yield	0.40	0.42	0.46	0.43
Rice (paddy)				
Production	2,511	2,384	2,236	2,441
Area planted	1,040	972	956	1,056
Yield	2.41	2.45	2.34	2.38
Maize (including Nili)				
Production	2,938	3,231	3,309	3,347
Area planted	1,885	1,906	1,924	1,935
Yield	1.56	1.70	1.72	1.73

Source: Ministry of Agriculture

PRODUCTION OF MAJOR AGRICULTURAL CROPS
(production in thousand metric tons; area planted in
thousands of feddans; yield in metric tons/feddan) 1/

Agricultural Year Ended October 31	1978/79	1979/80	1980/81	1981/82
Sugarcane				
Production	8,791	8,618	8,805	8,603
Area planted	249	252	251	254
Yield	35.35	34.14	35.09	33.18
Groundnuts				
Production	27	26	26	24
Area planted	31	28	28	29
Yield	0.87	0.90	0.90	0.82
Fruits & Vegetables				
Citrus fruits				
Production	1,216	1,067	1,033	1,490
Area planted	190	198	198	2.1
Dates				
Production	406	446	391	440
Area planted	33	34	34	33
Other fruits				
Production	751	768	850	930
Area planted	150	163	170	180
Potatoes				
Production	1,019	1,214	1,195	1,184
Area planted	142	167	159	153
Yield	7.2	7.3	7.5	7.7
Other vegetables				
Production	6,755	6,747	6,829	6,981
Area plantd	873	878	868	882

1/ Production may not always equal the product of area planted
and yield because of rounding.
2/ Excludes crops consumed green (as vegetables and forage).
3/ Winter (export) crop only.

Table 52.
INDICES OF AGRICULTURAL PRODUCTION AND YIELD
(1974/75 = 100)

Agricultural Year ended October 31	1977/78	1978/79	1979/80	1980/81	1981/82
Production					
Wheat	95.1	91.3	88.3	95.3	99.2
Horsebeans 1/	98.7	100.9	91.0	88.9	111.1
Onions 2/	97.4	68.6	135.8	143.2	129.2
Cotton (lint)	114.7	126.7	138.5	141.1	129.2
Rice (paddy)	97.0	103.6	98.4	92.3	100.7
Maize (+ Nili)	112.1	105.6	116.2	119.0	120.3
Millet (sorghum)	87.9	81.9	82.8	84.2	76.9
Sugarcane	105.0	111.2	109.1	111.4	108.9
Groundnuts	93.9	97.5	93.9	93.9	86.6
Citrus Fruits	97.8	120.0	105.3	102.0	147.1
Dates	90.8	97.8	107.5	94.2	106.0
Other Fruits	112.0	117.3	120.0	132.8	145.3
Potatoes	107.2	141.5	168.6	165.9	164.4
Other Vegetables	109.6	116.5	116.3	117.7	120.4
Yield					
Wheat	95.9	91.1	92.5	95.2	100.7
Horsebeans	102.1	100.0	91.6	91.6	100.0
Onions	89.4	78.7	98.7	96.9	94.5
Cotton	129.9	142.6	149.6	161.3	152.1
Rice (paddy)	99.1	104.8	106.5	101.7	103.5
Maize (+ Nili)	107.9	102.6	111.8	113.2	113.8
Millet (sorghum)	99.4	98.7	99.4	100.0	98.7
Sugarcane	92.4	97.6	94.3	96.9	93.4
Groundnuts	95.4	100.0	103.4	103.4	94.2
Potatoes	82.2	98.6	99.4	103.0	106.0

1/ Excludes crops consumed green (as vegetables and forage)
2/ Winter (export) crop only

Source: Ministry of Agriculture

Table 53.

DEMAND AND SUPPLY DEVELOPMENT
FOR PRINCIPAL AGRICULTURAL COMMODITIES
(average annual % change)

1974-81

	Per Capita Demand	Total Demand	Domestic Supply	Demand-Supply Gap
Basic Food Commodities				
Wheat	3.8	6.4	0.6	5.8
Maize	3.9	6.4	3.5	2.9
Sugar	8.9	11.6	2.6	9.0
Beans	-0.2	2.3	-1.6	3.9
Lentils	1.4	3.8	-29.0	32.8
Edible Oils	4.6	7.2	0.6	6.6
Exportable Field Crops				
Cotton	4.2	6.8	1.8	5.0
Rice	0.3	2.8	1.5	1.3
Onions (winter)	2.5	4.9	1.3	3.6
Groundnuts	2.9	6.1	3.9	2.2
Fruits & Vegetables				
Citrus	-0.5	2.0	1.4	0.6
Potatoes	5.9	8.5	7.9	0.6
Tomatoes	2.5	5.1	5.1	0.0
Livestock Products				
Red Meat	3.8	6.4	1.8	4.6
Poultry	7.2	9.9	2.8	7.1
Fish	10.2	13.0	4.5	8.5
Milk	4.9	7.5	1.6	5.9

Source: Ministry of Agriculture

Table 54.

TRADE PERFORMANCE AND SELF-SUFFICIENCY FOR PRINCIPAL AGRICULTURAL COMMODITIES

(exports, imports in thousand tons; self-sufficiency in domestic supply or % of total domestic consumption)

	1974		1981	
	Exports (+) Imports (-)	Self Sufficiency	Exports (+) Imports (-)	Self Sufficiency
Basic Food Commodities				
Wheat	-3,200	36.8	-5,878	24.8
Rice	+136	111.2	+25	101.7
Maize	-388	86.6	-1,300	71.1
Sugar	-23	96.0	-580	53.2
Beans	-10	92.5	-90	69.8
Lentils	-13	81.2	-85	5.6
Edible Oils	-151	49.7	-355	31.6
Other Exportable Field Crops				
Cotton	+232	211.0	+165	149.6
Onions (fresh)	+104	150.0	+40	117.0
Groundnuts	+7.4	12.6	+7.5	18.0
Livestock Products				
Red Meat	-1	99.7	-125	73.3
Poultry	-1	99.2	-60	62.8
Fish	-19	92.4	-130	53.6
Milk	-138	92.5	-1,150	62.2
Fruits & Vegetables				
Citrus	+162	120.3	+140	114.0
Potatoes	+100	118.2	+145	113.6
Tomatoes	+2	100.1	+3	100.1

Source: Ministry of Agriculture, 1983

Table 55.

PRINCIPAL CROP PRODUCTION (1980/81)

Crop	Area Planted ('000 feddans)	Production ('000 metric tons)
Wheat	1,400	1,938
Horsebeans	238	208
Onions (export crop only)	19	154
Berseem (clover)	2,778	
Cotton	1,178	539
Rice (paddy)	956	2,236
Maize	1,924	3,309
Millet	413	653
Sugarcane (1979/80)	252	8,618
Groundnuts	28	26
Citrus Fruits	198	1,033
Dates	34	391
Other Fruits	170	350
Potatoes	160	1,210
Other Vegetables	868	6,829

Source: Ministry of Agriculture

Table 56.

MEAT AND POULTRY PRODUCTION
(thousand metric tons)

	1976	1977	1978	1979	1980	1981*	1982*
Meat	307	315	321	330	336	343	348
Cattle	121	123	125	127	131	131	133
Buffalo	130	131	134	139	140	143	146
Sheep	32	37	38	39	40	42	43
Goats	17	17	17	18	18	19	19
Swine	2	2	2	2	2	2	2
Camels	5	5	5	5	5	5	5
Poultry	115	121	115	119	136	140	142
Total	422	436	436	449	472	482	490

* Preliminary

Source: Ministry of Agriculture

Table 57.

BILATERAL TREATIES IN FORCE EGYPT/USA

Agricultural Commodities

Description:	Treaty	Date Signed (Amendments)
Agricultural Commodities Agreement, with exchange of notes.	12 UST 1240 TIAS 4884 UNTS 251 (13 UST 1661) (TIAS 4982) (445 UNTS 374)	Sept. 2, 1961 (March 28, 1962)
Agricultural Commodities Agreement, with exchange of notes.	13 UST 121 TIAS 4947 UNTS 107 (13 UST 1921) (TIAS 5449) (460 UNTS 340)	Feb. 10, 1962 (Sept. 1, 1962)
Agricultural Commodities Agreement, with exchange of notes.	13 UST 2166 TIAS 5179 UNTS 39 (15 UST 1676) (TIAS 5179) (UNTS 396)	Oct. 8, 1962 (July 20, 1964)
Agricultural Commodities Agreement, with exchange of notes.	17 UST 17 TIAS 5951 579 UNTS 83	Jan. 3, 1966
Agricultural Commodities Agreement, with exchange of notes.	17 UST 6 TIAS 5950 579 UNTS 63	Jan. 3, 1966
Agricultural Commodities Agreement, with exchange of notes.	25 UST 1245 TIAS 7855 (26 UST 1915) (TIAS 8147)	June 7, 1974 June 30, 1975
Most recent related agreement		Dec. 21, 1981
Agricultural Commodities Agreement, with annexes.	TIAS 9683 (TIAS 10089)	March 20, 1979 June 28, 1981

Source: Treaties in Force, United Nations

Table 58.

LIVESTOCK POPULATION
(thousands)

	1979	1980	1981
Cattle	1,965	1,912	1,912
Buffaloes	2,321	2,347	2,347
Sheep	1,679	1,593	1,599
Goats	1,427	1,451	1,451
Pigs	15*	15*	15*
Horses	12	9	9*
Asses	1,672	1,706	1,746*
Camels	99	99	84
Chickens	27,292	27,597	27,903
Ducks	3,440	3,489	3,538*
Turkeys	733	742	751*

*FAO estimates

Source: FAO Yearbook 1983

Table 59.

AGRICULTURE SECTOR DEVELOPMENT: SOME KEY INDICATORS

	1960	1970	1980
Share of Agriculture in Total Value Added (%)	27.9	25.3	20.0
Agricultural Exports as % of Total Exports	33.0	25.0	9.0
Overall Agricultural Trade Balance ($ million, current prices)	225.0	300.0	-2,500.0
Land/Population Ratio (feddans per person) *	0.21	0.18	0.15

* 1 feddan = 1.038 acres

Source: Ministry of Agriculture

TRADE

Table 60.

BALANCE OF PAYMENTS
(% of GDP)

	1974	1979	1980/81	1981/82	Estimate 1982/83
Current Account Receipts	23.1	45.4	47.5	41.2	40.4
of which:					
Non-oil exports	14.1	6.4	4.8	4.4	4.3
Other	9.0	39.0	42.7	36.8	36.1
of which:					
Oil exports	2.3	15.6	19.2	18.5	15.1
Workers' remittances	1.7	13.5	12.2	7.6	10.6
Suez Canal	0.0	3.2	3.2	3.6	3.5
Tourism	2.4	3.3	2.9	2.5	2.0
Current Account Payments	37.5	56.0	57.6	55.0	48.4
of which:					
Merchandise imports	32.6	43.1	44.1	41.0	35.2
Consumer goods	13.7	15.3	16.4	14.9	12.3
Intermdediate goods	13.6	11.6	11.6	13.5	12.6
Capital goods	5.3	16.1	16.1	12.6	10.2
Interest payments	0.7	1.3	3.2	3.6	3.9
Profits transferred abroad	0.5	5.2	5.6	5.3	4.9
Current Account Deficit	14.4	10.6	10.0	13.8	8.0
Medium & Long-term Capita	0.6	13.9	9.7	9.1	8.5
Official grants & loans	0.2	4.1	4.4	3.7	3.0
Medium & Long-term Debt, Disbursed & Outstanding	36.1	62.9	58.3	59.1	53.6

Source: Ministry of Finance

Table 61.

BALANCE OF PAYMENTS SUMMARY
(billion US $)

	1980/81	1981/82	Estimated 1982/83
Exports of goods and services	11.1	10.4	11.5
of which: oil (Egypt's share)	3.2	3.3	2.8
: remittances	2.9	1.9	2.9
Imports of goods and services	-13.5	-13.9	-13.7
of which: merchandise	-10.3	-10.4	-9.8
Current account balance	-2.3	-3.5	-2.2
Medium- and long-term capital flows	2.3	2.3	2.4
Unallocated	-0.1	0.6	0.7
Overall balance	-0.2	-0.6	0.9

Source: Ministry of Finance and independent estimates

Table 62.

TRADE BY COMMODITY SECTIONS
(% of total)

	1976	1977	1978	1979	1980
Exports					
Food, Beverages & Tobacco	19.3	18.0	15.2	9.2	6.4
Raw Materials	29.5	30.9	27.5	26.5	17.6
Fuels	25.0	24.2	27.7	41.6	64.2
Manufactured Goods	26.0	26.9	29.5	22.7	11.7
Imports					
Food, Beverages & Tobacco	25.3	21.0	23.1	22.5	27.8
Raw Materials	8.8	11.3	8.9	9.7	11.5
Fuels	5.7	2.3	1.5	.8	1.1
Manufactured Goods	60.2	65.3	66.4	66.9	59.6

Source: International Financial Statistics Supplement on Trade

Table 63.
BALANCE OF PAYMENTS – CURRENT ACCOUNT
(million US $)

	1978	1979	1980/81	1981/82
Trade Balance	**-3,440**	**-3,830**	**-4,717**	**-4,601**
Merchandise Exports, f.o.b.	2,558	3,987	5,617	5,779
Petroleum	1,262	2,825	4,489	4,669
Egypt	(802)	(1,878)	(3,179)	(3,329)
Foreign companies	(460)	(947)	(1,310)	(1,340)
Non-Petroleum	1,296	1,162	1,128	1,110
Cotton	(286)	(348)	(330)	(380)
Other agriculture	(223)	(200)	(210)	(190)
Textiles	(272)	(280)	(290)	(280)
Other manufactures	(515)	(334)	(298)	(260)
Merchandise Imports, c.i.f.	-5,998	-7,817	-10,334	-10,380
Wheat and flour	-841	-792	-1,086	-1,130
Other agriculture	-696	-990	-1,610	-1,550
Intermediate goods	-1,673	-2,113	-2,707	-3,425
Petroleum	(-149)	(-243)	(-335)	(-505)
Other int. goods	(-1,524)	(-1,870)	(-2,372)	(-2,920)
Capital goods	-2,022	-2,921	-3,781	-3,175
Domestic companies	(-1,700)	(-2,390)	(-3,131)	(-2,475)
Foreign companies	(-322)	(-531)	(-650)	(-700)
Manufactured cons. goods	-766	-1,001	-1,150	-1,100
Net Non-factor Services	**927**	**540**	**1,116**	**898**
Receipts	1,541	1,414	2,186	2,183
Tourism	702	601	712	611
Suez Canal	514	589	780	909
Other n.f.s. receipts	325	224	694	663
Payments	-614	-964	-1,078	-1,285
Resource balance	-2,513	-3,380	-3,601	-3,703
Net Factor Services	**1,098**	**1,376**	**1,190**	**151**
Receipts	1,905	2,751	3,259	2,403
Workers' remittances	1,761	2,445	2,855	1,935
Other n.s. receipts	144	306	404	468
Payments	-807	-1,375	-2,069	-2,252
Interests-official	-314	-150	-759	-912
Interests-private	-72	-86	n.a.	NA
Profits transf. abroad	-392	-947	-1,310	-1,340
Other f.s. payments	-29	-192	n.a.	NA
Net Private Transfers	**54**	**89**	**63**	**51**
Current Account Balance	**-1,361**	**-1,195**	**-2,348**	**-3,501**
Current account receipts	6,058	8,241	11,125	10,416
Current account payments	-7,419	-10,156	-13,473	-13,917

Source: Ministry of Finance and IMF

Table 64.
BALANCE OF PAYMENTS - CAPITAL ACCOUNT
(million US$)

	1978	1979	1980/81	1981/82
Autonomous				
Non-monetary Capital	1,528	2,527	2,280	2,315
Direct investment	387	1,516	1,036	1,325
Official loans & grants (net)	1,028	749	1,020	945
Disbursements	(1,202)	(997)	(1,402)	(1,419)
Repayments	(-174)	(-248)	(-382)	(-474)
Private loans (net)	113	262	224	45
Suppliers' credit	83	253	234	65
Disbursements	(684)	(823)	(1,174)	(1,050)
Repayments	(-601)	(-570)	(-940)	(-985)
Other (net)	30	9	-10	-20
Balance on Autonomous Transactions	167	612	-68	-1,186
Medium-term Balance of Payments Financing	809	72	--	--
Grants	291	72	--	--
Loans	518	--	--	--
Balance on Non-monetary Transactions	976	684	-68	-1,186
Unallocated	-504	-377	-82	571*
Monetary capital	-472	-307	150	615
Commercial banks	-494	-101	170	910
Central Bank (net)	22	-206	-20	-295
Official loans and deposits	-9	-9		
Bilateral payments	-35	-59		
Reserves	14	-98		
IMF (net)	52	-40		

* Includes $295 million in financing by foreign currency banks corresponding mainly to the new foreign currency reserve requirement.

Source: Central Bank of Egypt and IMF

Table 65.

MAIN COMMODITIES TRADED
(million LE)

Exports

	1979	1980	1981	1982
Raw Cotton	267.3	296.4	320.0	286.0
Cotton Yarn	130.1	135.9	108.6	86.6
Crude Oil	396.5	1,233.3	1,233.5	1,211.2
Oil Products	138.9	137.3	223.8	235.5
Cotton Woven Goods	56.0	56.2	39.2	30.2
Oranges	14.4	27.2	33.0	36.8
Potatoes	18.8	22.7	17.9	28.8
Bleached Rice	NA	NA	28.7	7.6
Aluminium Ingots	NA	NA	77.8	46.2

Imports

	1979	1980	1981	1982
Wheat	174.3	308.9	531.2	492.2
Wheat Flour	68.4	71.7	250.8	192.2
Maize	31.3	71.7	219.9	210.1
Dairy	49.2	78.1	150.9	117.2
Tobacco	60.5	49.4	65.0	79.9
Fats & Vegetable oils	75.0	79.7	84.6	108.7
Chemicals & Condensates	103.8	166.7	138.4	221.5
Cars	83.7	83.5	133.1	178.0
Iron Bars	122.8	206.8	192.4	212.8
Capital goods & machinery	832.9	832.9	1,588.2	1,682.4
Refined sugur	NA	NA	164.4	250.1
Cement	NA	NA	164.9	250.1

Sources: Central Agency for Mobilization and Statistics; National Bank of Egypt, Economic Bulletin

Table 66.

MAIN TRADING PARTNERS
(% of total)

Exports to:

	1980	1981	1982
Italy	39.6	25.6	22.1
USA	7.7	3.8	4.7
West Germany	7.6	2.3	4.0
Netherlands	5.8	4.1	5.4
USSR	4.2	4.1	4.3
UK	3.2	1.3	2.4
Japan	2.6	4.9	2.5
Yugoslavia	2.1	1.4	1.7
Saudi Arabia	1.8	2.5	2.8
France	1.7	3.2	6.9
Romania	3.6	2.6	5.9
China	1.8	2.1	1.1
Sudan	NA	0.4	2.1

Imports from:

	1980	1981	1982
USA	19.3	19.6	19.0
France	10.2	9.4	7.5
West Germany	9.4	10.2	9.9
Italy	6.7	7.4	7.6
UK	6.1	4.9	4.4
Japan	4.7	4.3	4.5
Rumania	3.2	3.2	2.2
Yugoslavia	2.2	1.2	1.5
Netherlands	2.0	3.1	3.5
USSR	1.6	2.6	1.9
Czechoslovakia	NA	0.9	1.5

Sources: National Bank of Egypt and Economic Bulletin, IMF

Table 67.

FOREIGN TRADE INDICATORS

	1977	1978	1979	1980	1981
Annual Percent Change, Imports	26.5	39.7	-43.0	26.7	80.7
Annual Percent Change, Exports	12.3	1.7	5.9	65.6	6.1
Balance of Trade	-3.11	-4.99	-2.00	-1.81	-5.55
Ratio of Exports to GDP	8.1	6.9	10.3	--	--
Ratio of Imports to GDP	23.0	26.9	21.5	--	--

Source: International Financial Statistics Supplement on Trade, 1982.

Table 68.

COMMODITY COMPOSITION OF EXPORTS
(million US$)

	1977	1978	1979	1980/81	1981/82
Petroleum					
Egypt	720	802	1,878	3,179	3,329
Partners	292	460	947	1,310	1,340
	1,012	1,262	2,825	4,489	4,669
Agricultural Goods					
Cotton	491	336	382	394	380
Rice	60	51	32	39	35
Citrus Fruit	55	53	21	47	54
Onions & Potatos	61	28	32	44	46
Others	59	91	65	95	105
	726	559	532	619	620
Industrial Goods					
Cotton	175	229	186	195	NA
Cotton textiles	122	126	92	69	280
Other weaving/textiles	38	55	55	70	NA
Food stuff	53	50	30	25	NA
Chemicals	49	43	23	8	260
Metal and eng.	37	92	109	72	NA
Others	147	102	280	301	NA
	621	697	775	740	540
Total Exports	2,359	2,518	4,132	5,848	5,829

Source: Egypt General Central Petroleum Corporation (EGPC) and Central Agency for Mobilization and Statistics (CAPMAS)

LABOR

Table 69.
EMPLOYMENT BY ECONOMIC SECTOR
('000s of Persons)

	1975	1976	1977	1978	1979	1980/81
Commodity Sectors	5,931	5,848	5,911	6,082	6,262	6,457
Agriculture	4,218	4,068	4,104	4,135	4,165	4,200
Industry, Petroleum & Mining	1,175	1,200	1,247	1,297	1,351	1,450
Electricity	41	47	48	52	53	63
Public Utilities	50	53	55	60	64	64
Construction	447	480	457	538	629	680
Distributive Sectors	1,371	1,429	1,495	1,543	1,578	1,677
Transportation, Comm. & Storage	404	415	444	449	452	460
Trade & Finance	967	1,014	1,051	1,094	1,126	1,217
Service Sectors	2,131	2,228	2,481	2,634	2,797	3,046
Housing	143	144	145	147	155	166
Other Services 1/	1,853	1,988	2,084	2,336	2,642	2,880
Total	9,433	9,505	9,887	10,259	10,637	11,180

* For 1978-1980/81, independent estimates assume annual growth rates of 6.5, 6.2 and 6.0 percent respectively.

Source: Ministry of Planning and independent estimates

Table 70.

DISTRIBUTION OF EMPLOYMENT

	1977		1981/82	
	('000)	%	('000)	%
Agriculture	4,103.5	41.5	4,247.5	36.2
Mining	29.0	0.3	39.5	0.3
Manufacturing	1,199.4	12.1	1,423.2	12.1
Oil & Oil Products	18.7	0.2	24.5	0.2
Electricity	48.0	0.5	64.2	0.6
Construction	457.0	4.6	664.1	5.7
Transportation & Communications	431.6	4.4	433.3	3.7
Suez Canal	12.6	0.1	18.8	0.2
Commerce	967.1	9.8	1.103.8	9.4
Finance	55.7	0.6	71.9	0.6
Insurance	9.6	0.1	13.6	0.1
Hotels & Restaurants	96.2	1.0	140.5	1.2
House Property	144.8	1.5	171.3	1.5
Public Utilities	54.6	0.5	66.2	0.6
Private and Social Services	765.4	7.7	895.6	7.6
Social Insurance	18.1	0.2	29.5	0.2
Government Services Sector	1,474.0	14.9	2,317.4	19.8
Total	9,885.3	100.0	11,724.9	100.0

Source: Five Year Plan

TRANSPORTATION & COMMUNICATIONS

Table 71.

TOURIST ACTIVITY
('000s of People)

	1978	1979	1980	1980/81
Arab countries	456	397	479	526
OECD countries	503	575	664	684
Socialist countries	25	31	24	24
Other	68	61	86	107
Total	1,052	1,064	1,253	1,341
Total Expenditure (mn LE)	491.1	420.6	455.2	498.2

Source: Middle East and North Africa 1983-84

Table 72.

INFRASTRUCTURE

Km of paved road	12,000
Km of railroad (standard gauge)	4,882
Telephones (1981)	532,020
Number of Radio Stations	30
Radios (1982)	6.5 million
Televisions in Use (1982)	1.9 million
Aggregate Circulation of Daily Papers (1982)	3,012,000
Registered Motor Vehicles (1981)	902,698

Source: MERI compiled.

Table 73.

SUEZ CANAL TRAFFIC AND REVENUES

	1976	1979	1980/81	1981/82
Number of Transits (thousands)	16.8	20.4	21.2	21.9
of which: Oil tankers	2.6	2.7	3.1	3.5
Net Tonnage (million tons)	187.7	266.2	308.0	353.4
of which: Oil tankers	77.9	86.3	110.6	135.4

Source: Suez Canal Authority

HEALTH, EDUCATION AND WELFARE

Table 74.

EDUCATIONAL ENROLLMENT

	1975	1978	1979	1980
Preceding 1st Level (under age 6)				
Total	41,948	59,050	67,913	74,921
Females (%)	49	50	49	49
Teaching Staff	n.a.	1,343	1,790	n.a.
First Level (age 6-11)				
Total	4,120,936	4,287,124	4,434,557	4,662,816
Females (%)	38	40	40	40
Gross Enrollment (%)	73	74	75	76
Teaching Staff	118,251	127,021	137,045	167,821
Second Level (age 12-17)				
Total /1	2,107,891	2,523,642	2,592,964	2,929,168
Females (%)	35	37	37	37
Gross Enrollment (%)	43	49	50	52
Teaching Staff	78,789	100,288	111,877	121,999
Third Level /2 (age 18-22)				
Total	455,097	486,067	502,884	n.a.
Females (%)	30	31	31	
Students in Technical Fields (%)	39	37	37	
Teaching Staff	n.a.	21,680	22,507	n.a.

/1 Figures do not include classes at Al Azhar University except for 1980
/2 Figures for 1978 and 1979 exclude non-university education and Al Azhar

Source: International Yearbook of Education, 1983 UNESCO

Table 75.

PUBLIC EXPENDITURE ON EDUCATION

	1975	1978	1979	1980
Total (in national currency, 000)	262,328	434,931	539,937	n.a.
Total as % of GDP	5	4.2	4.1	n.a.

Source: International Yearbook of Education, 1983 UNESCO

Table 76.

HEALTH INDICATORS

	1976	1977	1978	1979	1980
Population per physician /1	1180	1190	1120	1040	970
Population per nursing person /2	1140	n.a.	1090	1320	1500

/1 Includes registered physicians not all of whom practice in the country
/2 Professional and assistant nurses only. 1980 figures include personnel in government service only.

Source: World Bank Social Data, 1983

For Product Safety Concerns and Information please contact our EU
representative GPSR@taylorandfrancis.com
Taylor & Francis Verlag GmbH, Kaufingerstraße 24, 80331 München, Germany

www.ingramcontent.com/pod-product-compliance
Lightning Source LLC
Chambersburg PA
CBHW071354290426
44108CB00014B/1546